Faith and Love in Ignatius of Antioch

Faith and Love in Ignatius of Antioch

OLAVI TARVAINEN

Translated by Jonathon Lookadoo

☙PICKWICK *Publications* · Eugene, Oregon

FAITH AND LOVE IN IGNATIUS OF ANTIOCH

Translation copyright © 2016 Jonathon Lookadoo. All rights reserved. Except for brief quotations in critical publications or reviews, no part of this book may be reproduced in any manner without prior written permission from the publisher. Write: Permissions, Wipf and Stock Publishers, 199 W. 8th Ave., Suite 3, Eugene, OR 97401.

This book is a translation of Olavi Tarvainen's *Glaube und Liebe bei Ignatius von Antiochien*, which first appeared as volume 14 in Series A of the Schriften der Luther-Agricola-Gesellschaft (Helsinki, 1967) and was published under the auspices of the Luther-Agricola Society. It is translated with permission.

Pickwick Publications
An Imprint of Wipf and Stock Publishers
199 W. 8th Ave., Suite 3
Eugene, OR 97401

www.wipfandstock.com

PAPERBACK ISBN: 978-1-5326-0129-3
HARDCOVER ISBN: 978-1-5326-0131-6
EBOOK ISBN: 978-1-5326-0130-9

Cataloguing-in-Publication data:

Names: Tarvainen, Olavi. | Lookadoo, Jonathan
Title: Faith and love in Ignatius of Antioch / Olavi Tarvainen, translated by Jonathan Lookadoo.
Description: Eugene, OR: Pickwick Publications, 2016 | Includes bibliographical references and index.
Identifiers: ISBN 978-1-5326-0129-3 (paperback) | ISBN 978-1-5326-0131-6 (hardcover) | ISBN 978-1-5326-0130-9 (ebook)
Subjects: LCSH: Ignatius, Saint, Bishop of Antioch, -approximately 110
Classification: BR65.I34 T18 2016 (print) | BR65.I34 (ebook)

Manufactured in the U.S.A.   11/07/16

None of these things escapes you if you direct faith and love, which are the beginning and the end of life, perfectly toward Jesus Christ. Faith is the beginning, love the end. But the two in unity are God. Everything else that belongs to virtue follows from that.

(IGNATIUS, *EPHESIANS* 14.1)

Contents

Translator's Preface | ix
Preface | xxi
Introduction | xxiii

1 Faith and Love as Central Themes of Ignatian Thought | 1
2 Faith | 10
3 Love | 59
   Conclusion | 86

Bibliography | 91
Author Index | 97
Ancient Document Index | 101

Translator's Preface

I first learned about Olavi Tarvainen's *Glaube und Liebe bei Ignatius von Antiochien* (*Faith and Love in Ignatius of Antioch*) through the footnotes of others who had written about Ignatius when I was initially researching for my Ph.D. proposal.[1] However, I did not have an opportunity to read the book until I found it in the Tübingen Theologicum while there for the Winter Semester of 2014–15. I was simultaneously reading Dietrich Bonhoeffer's *Widerstand und Ergebung* as part of a theological German reading course.[2] I enjoyed sharing, perhaps too much, the connections that I was trying to draw between Ignatius of Antioch, Martin Luther, and Dietrich Bonhoeffer on various points of Christology, faith, and suffering. When I noticed Tarvainen's comparisons of Ignatius with Luther on faith and love, I wondered if his slim volume might still have something to say to an Anglophone audience. Happily, the folk at Pickwick Publishers were kind enough to help me find out. Yet it remains to say something about why a book that is nearly fifty years old should be translated into English.

---

1. Olavi Tarvainen, *Glaube und Liebe bei Ignatius von Antiochien* (Schriften der Luther-Agricola-Gesellschaft 14; Helsinki: Luther-Agricola-Gesellschaft, 1967). All notes in the translator's preface will contain full bibliographic material to avoid anachronism in bibliography of Tarvainen's study.

2. Dietrich Bonhoeffer, *Widerstand und Ergebung: Briefe und Aufzeichnungen aus der Haft* (Gütersloh: Gütersloher Verlagshaus, 1951). I am grateful to Evan Graber and Thom Finley for their interest and stimulating conversations during our walks along Wilhelmstraße.

Translator's Preface

The primary reasons for translating this book pertain to those who will read Tarvainen as students of Ignatius and early Christian theology. *Faith and Love* remains a valuable but underread volume in such circles. To my knowledge, Tarvainen's study remains the only stand-alone treatment of faith and love in Ignatius of Antioch, and it uses this potent juxtaposition of terms as a lens through which to view Ignatius's thought holistically, yielding an intriguing, exciting, and largely compelling picture of Ignatius's theology. He offers a generous reading of Ignatius that situates him within the stream of Pauline and Johannine tradition. Tarvainen likewise traces certain thoughts from Ignatius's letters into later Christian texts and may invite readers of this book to further this project. More can be said about these merits of Tarvainen's book for those who will read the book alongside Ignatius and other Ignatian scholarship.

Perhaps the most enduring consideration to be noted in Tarvainen's favor is that his book remains the only monograph-length study of faith and love in Ignatius. Whatever flaws may exist in Tarvainen's work, it ought to be read for this reason alone. This is not to say that others have not examined faith and love in Ignatius.[3] In addition to studies that preceded Tarvainen,[4] recent articles have probed Ignatius's understanding of the faith of Christ (πίστις Χριστοῦ),[5] shown that love is closely associated with the concept

---

3. These words are juxtaposed in Ignatius's letters at *Eph.* 1.1; 9.1; 14.1–2; 20.1; *Magn.* 1.2; 5.2; 6.1; 13.1; *Trall.* 8.1; *Rom.* inscr.; *Phld.* 9.2; 11.2; *Smyrn.* inscr.; 1.1; 6.1; 13.2; *Pol.* 6.2.

4. E.g., Eduard von der Goltz, *Ignatius als Christ und Theologe* (Leipzig: Hinrichs, 1894) 41–47; Jean Colson, "Agapè chez Ignace d'Antioche," in *Studia Patristica* 3 (ed. Frank Leslie Cross; Berlin: Akademie, 1961) 341–53.

5. Ferdinando Bergamelli, "'Fede di Gesù Cristo' nelle lettere di Ignazio di Antiochia," *Salesianum* 66 (2004) 649–64; Mark W. Elliott, "Πίστις Χριστοῦ in the Church Fathers and Beyond," in *The Faith of Jesus Christ: The Pistis Christou Debate—Exegetical, Biblical, and Theological Studies* (eds. Michael F. Bird and Preston M. Sprinkle; Milton Keynes, UK: Paternoster, 2009) 279–90, here at 281–82; Michael R. Whitenton, "After ΠΙΣΤΙΣ ΧΡΙΣΤΟΥ: Neglected Evidence from the Apostolic Fathers," *Journal of Theological Studies* 61 (2010) 82–109, here at 87, 91–100.

Translator's Preface

of life,[6] and offered the intriguing proposal that Ignatius connects faith with flesh and incarnation and links love to spirit and the passion in *Trall.* 8.1.[7] Vall offers the lengthiest treatment of the topic since Tarvainen and usefully guides readers from the way in which each concept functions individually to their place in Ignatius's teleological understanding of God's economy.[8]

Yet for all these additions, Tarvainen devotes the whole study to faith and love in Ignatius. He begins by analyzing two of Ignatius's most striking statements about faith and love to illustrate the importance of the concepts in his letters.[9] First, Ignatius claims that faith and love are everything and that nothing is better than these things (*Smyrn.* 6.1). More strikingly, Ignatius claims that the two in unity are God (τὰ δὲ δύο ἐν ἑνότητι γενομένα θεός ἐστιν; *Eph.* 14.1). Given Ignatius's propensity to connect words in surprising ways using a copulative verb,[10] it is doubtful that this latter phrase strictly identifies God as faith and love.[11] More likely is Tarvainen's suggestion that God is present in the outworking of faith and love.[12] Even if Tarvainen is wrong, though, his work on

---

6. Sergio Zañartu, "Les concepts de vie et de mort chez Ignace d'Antioche," *Vigiliae Christianae* 33 (1979) 324–41, here at 329–30.

7. Richard A. Bower, "The Meaning of ΕΠΙΤΥΓΧΑΝΩ in the Epistles of St. Ignatius of Antioch," *Vigiliae Christianae* 28 (1974) 1–14, here at 10–11.

8. Gregory Vall, *Learning Christ: Ignatius of Antioch and the Mystery of Redemption* (Washington, DC: Catholic University of America Press, 2013) 159–99.

9. See chapter 1 of this volume.

10. E.g. Ignatius uses a relative pronoun + ἐστιν in *Eph.* 9.1; 14.1; 17.2; 18.1; 20.2; *Magn.* 7.1; 8.2; 10.2; 15; *Trall.* 6.1; 8.1; 11.2; *Phld.* inscr. See further, Graydon F. Snyder, "The Text and Syntax of Ignatius ΠΡΟΣ ΕΦΕΣΙΟΥΣ 20:2c," *Vigiliae Christianae* 22 (1968) 8–13, here at 9–10.

11. José Pablo Martin, "La pneumatologia en Ignacio de Antioquia," *Salesianum* 33 (1971) 379–454, here at 386.

12. Similarly, Robert M. Grant, *Ignatius of Antioch* (The Apostolic Fathers: A New Translation and Commentary 4; Camden: Thomas Nelson, 1966) 44–45; William R. Schoedel, *Ignatius of Antioch* (Hermeneia; Philadelphia: Fortress, 1985) 76; Mikael Isacson, *To Each Their Own Letter: Structure, Themes, and Rhetorical Strategies in the Letters of Ignatius of Antioch* (ConBNT 42; Stockholm: Almqvist and Wiksell International, 2004) 61.

this and other Ignatian passages concerning faith and love is worthy of study by virtue of the close textual work that lies behind the book. By studying faith and love in the context of Ignatius's letters, he avoids abstracting the concepts from their contexts.[13] In this respect, the book lives up to its title. Tarvainen's monograph on faith and love studies the two words as they are used by Ignatius.

Tarvainen then employs faith and love as lenses through which to view the rest of Ignatius's letters as he focuses chapters 2 and 3 on faith and love individually. His reading of Ignatius takes into account an expansive definition of faith that is primarily drawn from Ignatius's letters. Ignatius's use of πίστις and related words contains propositional elements, particularly in *Philadelphians* and *Smyrneans*.[14] He opens the letter to Smyrna by commending the completeness of the Smyrneans' faith and soon after praises them for being convinced that Jesus is David's descendant and Son of God, that he was born of a virgin and baptized by John, and that he was crucified and resurrected (*Smyrn.* 1.1–2).[15] In Philadelphia, Ignatius counters the doubt that some have in the gospel by insisting both that the gospel is to be found in the archives and that Jesus truly defines the archives in his death and resurrection (*Phld.* 8.2). For this reason, the gospel is worthy of belief. Tarvainen links these propositional connotations to a broader discussion of Ignatius's opponents and unity in the church, but throughout the discussion he comes back to Ignatius's emphasis on the right faith.[16]

Faith has a strong relational component in Ignatius's letters that can be found in him, his readers, and God. Ignatius wishes

---

13. Richard Hays has offered a recent critique of those who would reduce theology to word study ("Humanity Prior to the Revelation of Faith," in *Beyond Bultmann: Reckoning a New Testament Theology* [ed. Bruce W. Longenecker and Mikeal C. Parsons; Waco: Baylor University Press, 2014], 61–77, here at 69–71).

14. Vall, *Learning*, 161; Teresa Morgan, *Roman Faith and Christian Faith: Pistis and Fides in the Early Roman Empire and Early Churches* (Oxford: Oxford University Press, 2015) 513–14.

15. Henri de Genouillac, *L'église chrétienne au temps de Saint Ignace d'Antioche* (Paris: Beauchesne, 1907) 115–16.

16. Chapter 2, section 1.

Translator's Preface

to demonstrate in his death that he is genuinely a Christian and is thereby faithful (*Rom.* 3.2). Likewise, Ignatius addresses his readers as "believers" (πιστοί; *Eph.* 21.2), that is, those who hold to their beliefs about Jesus such that it is evident in their corporate life and unity.[17] God is also faithful in Jesus to answer requests (*Trall.* 13.3). Finally, Jesus demonstrates faithfulness principally in his death and resurrection (*Eph.* 20.1; *Phld.* 8.2).[18] Tarvainen's broad understanding of faith fits Ignatius's use of the πίστις-lexicon, while simultaneously allowing him to engage traditional Ignatian enigmas under the rubric of faith.

Tarvainen demonstrates similar breadth in the question of Ignatian influences. He connects Paul with Ignatius's understanding of faith and John with Ignatius's depiction of love. He does not dwell on the question of which documents Ignatius may have known. More can certainly be said about what other early Christian texts Ignatius knew and how he may have known them.[19] However, if Tarvainen

---

17. What Paul Trebilco writes about New Testament texts continues to be true in Ignatius's letters. "[B]oundaries are *now* drawn between 'the believing ones' and 'the ones who do not believe'" (*Self-Designations and Group Identity in the New Testament* [Cambridge: Cambridge University Press, 2011], 120). Italics original.

18. Ian G. Wallis, *The Faith of Jesus Christ in Early Christian Traditions* (SNTSMS 84; Cambridge: Cambridge University Press, 1995) 190–91; Bergamelli, "Fede," 652–60; Whitenton, "After," 94–96; Morgan, *Roman Faith*, 513.

19. E.g. William R. Inge, "Ignatius," in *The New Testament in the Apostolic Fathers* (ed. A Committee of the Oxford Society of Historical Theology; Oxford: Clarendon, 1905) 63–83; Paul Foster, "The Epistles of Ignatius of Antioch and the Writings that Later Formed the New Testament," in *The Reception of the New Testament in the Apostolic Fathers* (eds. Andrew F. Gregory and Christopher M. Tuckett; Oxford: Oxford University Press, 2005) 159–86. On Paul, see Andreas Lindemann, "Paul's Influence on 'Clement' and Ignatius," in *Trajectories through the New Testament and the Apostolic Fathers* (eds. Andrew F. Gregory and Christopher M. Tuckett; Oxford: Oxford University Press, 2005) 9–24; Judith M. Lieu, "The Battle for Paul in the Second Century," *Irish Theological Quarterly* 75 (2010) 3–14; Jennifer R. Strawbridge, *The Pauline Effect: The Use of the Pauline Epistles by Early Christian Writers* (Studies of the Bible and Its Reception 5; Berlin: de Gruyter, 2015). On John, see Charles E. Hill, *The Johannine Corpus in the Early Church* (Oxford: Oxford University Press, 2004) 421–43; Titus Nagel, *Die Rezeption des Johannesevangeliums im 2. Jahrhundert: Studien zur vorirenäischen Auslegung des vierten Evangeliums*

Translator's Preface

is right that Ignatius knew something of the theological traditions that followed from Paul and John, then Tarvainen's analysis may be seen as an illustration of how Ignatius may have integrated their language and thought into his letters. Tarvainen emphasizes Paul's contribution to Ignatius's understanding of faith and John's impact on his notion of love, but he notes Pauline conceptions of love and Johannine understandings of faith as well. In particular, Paul's humility is cited in relation to the love of Paul and Ignatius for their respective churches, while John's stress on the incarnation is referenced in opposition to the docetic opponents' challenge to Ignatius's understanding of faith.[20] In spite of the occasional overgeneralization, Tarvainen rightly notes that faith and love go hand in hand for Paul, John, and Ignatius. His particular understanding of the way in which thematic and verbal similarities should be illustrated requires sharpening by more recent scholarship, but the impact of Paul and John runs more deeply through Ignatius's letters than direct citations alone can show. This element of Tarvainen's contribution remains defensible in current Ignatian scholarship.

Although Tarvainen's work is best characterized as historical theology focused on a second-century figure, he looks forward to note ways in which later authors speak similarly to Ignatius. While studying Ignatius's reminder to the Smyrneans that no one should be prideful when given a position in the church (*Smyrn.* 6.1), Tarvainen mentions that the canons of the Nicaean Council record that certain deacons continued to usurp their position by distributing

---

in christlicher und christlich-gnostischer Literatur (Arbeiten zur Bibel und ihrer Geschichte 2; Leipzig: Evangelische Verlagsanstalt, 2000) 207–51; Allen Brent, "History and Eschatological Mysticism in Ignatius of Antioch," *Ephemerides Theologicae Lovanienses* 65 (1989) 309–29; Allen Brent, *Ignatius of Antioch and the Second Sophistic* (Studien und Texte zu Antike und Christentum 36; Tübingen: Mohr Siebeck, 2006) 26–29, 137–39.

20. See chapter 3, section 2 and chapter 2, section 1, respectively. If Paul's language has impacted Ignatius's understanding of humility (e.g. *Rom.* 9.2; 1 Cor 15.8-9) this may add an additional piece of evidence for Thomas A. Robinson's argument that Ignatius's repeated statements of unworthiness (*Eph.* 21.2; *Magn.* 14.1; *Trall.* 13.1; *Smyrn.* 11.1) do not stem from an intra-church crisis in Antioch (*Ignatius of Antioch and the Parting of the Ways: Early Jewish-Christian Relations* [Peabody: Hendrickson, 2009], 177–81).

Translator's Preface

or partaking in the Eucharist prior to their place in the order.[21] In contrast, Ignatius's command to love should bring about humility in Smyrna. Tarvainen likewise argues along Augustinian lines that Ignatius is concerned not only for unity in particular church communities but throughout the church in every place.[22] However, Martin Luther is the later theological figure who appears most often within the pages of the book. The comparison with Luther is of particular note because both Ignatius and Luther appeal especially to faith and love.[23] Luther claims that the Christian lives in Christ and in the neighbor. Faith enables life in Christ, while love enables life in the neighbor.[24] In his preface to the German mass, Luther understands

---

21. "It has come to the holy and great synod that in some districts and cities, the deacons give the eucharist to the presbyters, as neither canon nor custom allows; those who do not have authority to offer give the body of Christ to those who do offer" (ἦλθεν εἰς τὴν ἁγίαν καὶ μεγάλην σύνοδον, ὅτι ἐν τισι τόποις καὶ πόλεσι, τοῖς πρεσβυτέροις τὴν εὐχαριστίαν οἱ διάκονοι διδόασιν, ὥσπερ οὔτε ὁ κανὼν οὔτε ἡ συνήθεια παρέδωκε, τοὺς ἐξουσίαν μὴ ἔχοντας προσφέρειν τοῖς προσφέρουσι διδόναι τὸ σῶμα τοῦ Χριστοῦ; Canon 18). He also mentions Canon 19 from Nicaea and Canon 15 from Chalcedon, both of which specify regulations for the ordination of deaconesses

22. E.g., "The members of Christ truly join themselves through love of unity, and they adhere to their head, that is, to Christ Jesus through the same love" (*Membra vero Christi per unitatis charitatem sibi copulantur, et per eamdem capiti suo cohaerent, quod est Christus Jesus*; Augustine, *Unit. eccl.* 2). Ignatius demonstrates some concern for unity among churches in other areas, particularly in regional greetings and prayers for the church in Antioch (*Eph.* 21.2; *Magn.* 14-15; *Trall.* 12.1; 13.1; *Rom.* 9.1-10.2; *Phld.* 10.1-11.2; *Smyrn.* 10.1; 11.1-12.1; *Pol.* 7.2-8.2). However, his primary focus in the letters is that the various churches should be unified with their own bishops.

23. On Luther's view of faith and love, see Gerhard Ebeling, *Luther: An Introduction to his Thought* (tr. R. A. Wilson; Philadelphia: Fortress, 1970) 159-74, trans. of *Luther: Einführung in sein Danken* (Tübingen: Mohr Siebeck, 1965) 178-97; Oswald Bayer, *Martin Luther's Theology: A Contemporary Interpretation* (tr. Thomas H. Trapp; Grand Rapids: Eerdmans, 2008) 288-90.

24. "From everything, the conclusion follows that a Christian person does not live in themselves but in Christ and in the neighbor, in Christ through faith and in the neighbor through love" ("Aus den allenn folget der beschluß, das eyn Christen mensch lebt nit ynn yhm selb, sondern ynn Christo und seynem nehsten, ynn Christo durch den glauben, ym nehsten durch die liebe"; Martin Luther, *D. Martin Luthers Werke: Kritische Gesamtausgabe* [120 vols.; Weimar: Hermann Böhlaus Nachfolger, 1883-2009] 7.38).

Translator's Preface

faith and love as the two things in which the entire Christian faith can be summarized.[25] For Ignatius and Luther, faith and love are indivisible, though Tarvainen notes that these citations from Luther differ from Ignatius because faith and love have different ends. While for Luther faith is directed toward Christ and love toward the neighbor, Ignatius sees both as leading to God (*Eph.* 9.1).[26]

Such a synchronic comparison is somewhat unusual in historical studies and risk the possibility of anachronism. Yet Tarvainen's remarks are insightful. They illustrate ways in which others who follow in similar traditions to Ignatius have formulated concepts that appear to be related. Such a perspective is often lacking in studies of Ignatius and invites a fuller reception history of the letters that could begin with a fresh analysis of the later recensions not merely to indicate which is the earliest but also to examine how various recensions read Ignatius. Moreover, a reception of Ignatius could also engage with how various later figures have treated the letters. Some of this is already in existence in scattered studies, but it deserves continued exploration. One way to push Tarvainen's project forward would be to consider Ignatius's foreshadowing not only of later proto-orthodox theology but also of those who enjoy a less respectable memory in Christian history.[27]

This last paragraph points to two further things that should be said about Tarvainen's study. First, it is not a perfect book. The dismissal of the hypothesis that Ignatius was arrested due to intrachurch conflicts deserves further argumentation.[28] Likewise, the easy acceptance of a date early in the second century has come under challenge since 1967, particularly with the works of Robert Joly, Reinhard Hübner, and Thomas Lechner.[29] It is, like all other

25. See note 1 in the conclusion.

26. See chapter 1.

27. E.g., Paul R. Gilliam "Ignatius of Antioch and the Arian Controversy" (Ph.D. diss., University of Edinburgh, 2011).

28. Tarvainen cites P. N. Harrison, *Polycarp's Two Epistles to the Philippians* (Cambridge: Cambridge University Press, 1936). See now Schoedel, *Ignatius*, 10–11.

29. Robert Joly, *Le Dossier d'Ignace d'Antioche* (Université libre de Bruxelles: Faculté de Philosophie et Lettres 69; Brussels: Éditions de l'Université de

Translator's Preface

books, a book of its time. The same is also true when Tarvainen speaks of Torah observance as an issue in Ignatius's opponents, which, although by no means absent from discussions,[30] has been judged increasingly less significant in recent years.[31] Yet this does not mean that it should be ignored.

The combination of the book's unique lens through which to view Ignatius's theology, impressive contributions, and various imperfections leads to the second point, namely, that Tarvainen's work should continue to be pushed forward. It may be that a fuller or updated study of faith and love should be undertaken or that one of Tarvainen's suggestions deserves further development. For example, Tarvainen employs the Old Testament in order to make sense of Ignatius while likewise noting Ignatius's strong statements against Judaism. How, if at all, do these sentiments sit together in Ignatius? Tarvainen may offer a way forward with his suggestion that images from the Old Testament are utilized and developed to suit Ignatius's needs.[32]

Tarvainen's study will not convince everyone, and at points it shows its age. Yet few academic studies are wholly up-to-date fifty years later. What remains remarkable about Tarvainen's is that it continues to have so much to say. For this reason, it deserves to be

---

Bruxelles, 1979); Reinhard M. Hübner, "Thesen zur Echtheit und Datierung der sieben Briefe des Ignatius von Antiochien," *Zeitschrift für Antikes Christentum* 1 (1997) 44–72; Thomas Lechner, *Ignatius adversus Valentinianos? Chronologische und theologiegeschichtliche Studien zu den Briefen des Ignatius von Antiochien* (Vigiliae Christianae Supplements 47; Leiden: Brill, 1999) 6–113. For extensive critique of these and other cases for the inauthenticity of Ignatius's letters, see *Ignatius of Antioch: A Martyr Bishop and the Origin of Episcopacy* (London: Continuum, 2007) 95–143.

30. E.g., Paul J. Donahue, "Jewish Christianity in the Letters of Ignatius of Antioch," *Vigiliae Christianae* 32 (1978) 81–93.

31. See two of the more recent treatments in Matti Myllykoski, "Wild Beasts and Rabid Dogs: The Riddle of the Heretics in the Letters of Ignatius of Antioch," in *Wild Beasts and Rabid Dogs: The Riddle of the Heretics in the Letters of Ignatius of Antioch* (ed. Jostein Ådna; Wissenschaftliche Untersuchungen zum Neuen Testament 183; Tübingen: Mohr Siebeck, 2005) 341–77; John W. Marshall, "The Objects of Ignatius' Wrath and Jewish Angelic Mediators," *The Journal of Ecclesiastical History* 56 (2005) 1–23.

32. See chapter 2, section 1.

Translator's Preface

translated and thoroughly engaged by English-speaking scholars and students.

Yet two further matters remain before concluding this preface. The first involves the translation itself. Tarvainen's use of "f." and "ff." after citations of page numbers has fallen out of fashion as a way of referencing biblical studies footnotes among many Anglophone publishers. With that in mind, I have tried to find the specific page ranges to which Tarvainen refers. I have attempted to err on the side of inclusivity and hope that I have not too greatly altered Tarvainen's notes. Readers will also note that I have not translated non-English citations in the footnotes. Although German and French citations are reasonably standard in academic theology, this choice is primarily due to my lack of facility with Scandinavian languages, particularly the Finish and Swedish texts that Tarvainen cites. Attempting to translate sources in the footnotes would have resulted in an unbalanced and inadequate translation. I hope readers can forgive my linguistic shortcomings.

Lastly, I would like to thank those who have helped this volume come into being. First of all, I am grateful to the Luther-Agricola Society and to Paavo Tarvainen, who jointly own the copyright to *Glaube und Liebe bei Ignatius von Antiochien* and have generously and efficiently arranged for permission to be given to this translation. Juha Leinonen was a most helpful correspondent in relaying information to the various parties involved. There are surely more people to whom I owe my gratitude in arranging for permission to be granted. I regret that I do not know their names, but I thank them all the same. From the side of Pickwick Publications, Robin A. Parry and Matthew Wimer have been extremely helpful in guiding this project to completion. Likewise, the University of Otago has provided a lovely environment in which to work, and the exchange that lies between the Otago Theology Department and the Evangelisches Stift in Tübingen was fortuitous in providing not only my first opportunity to read Tarvainen but also a chance to improve my German. Finally, this translation would not have been completed without the support and encouragement

Translator's Preface

of my family. To my mother and father, Joel, Chantelle, Chloe, and especially to my wife, Jieun, I am extremely grateful.

Dunedin, September 2016
Jonathon Lookadoo

Preface

The current study considers a discipline that is rarely studied in Finland and the Nordic countries, namely, the discipline of Patristics. After I had previously occupied myself above all with Luther and with the Finish revival movements, my interest was kindled in the time of Christian antiquity, in the time in which the common spiritual heritage of the church, *theologia patristica*, emerges. The martyr-bishop Ignatius of Antioch, with whose thought I had already previously made my acquaintance, appeared to me to offer himself as a rewarding object of study because of his impressive personage and the continuing effects of his interpretation of the message of Christian faith.

On my overseas study trips I have had the opportunity to learn about adept patristic research elsewhere and to use foreign university libraries. I now have the enjoyable duty to give thanks to famous scholars in this discipline for the advice and suggestions that I have received in conversation with them. Of these, I would like above all to mention Professors Henry Chadwick in Oxford, Hans Freiherr von Campenhausen in Heidelberg, and Peter Meinhold in Kiel. My thanks are also due to Bishop Dr. Eino Sormunen, who has read through the manuscript of this work and given me valuable suggestions.

I thank Ms. Elke Mathias for the German translation of this work. Hanna Jaakkola, M. Phil., has helped me with proofreading. The Luther-Agricola Society has received the work in its monograph series. The State Classical Committee has offered a stipend

Preface

for this academic work, for which I would like to express my gratitude in this place.

Joensuu, September 1967
Olavi Tarvainen

Introduction

The end of the apostolic time signifies a deep gash in the history of Christianity. The men and women who saw the Lord with their own eyes, heard his words themselves, and were together with him during the time of his earthly journey are no longer living. The post-apostolic time now follows—the time of the Apostolic Fathers. However, the Apostolic Fathers no longer speak and write with the same spiritual authority as the New Testament authors. Instead, they occupy a place as mediators and defenders of the Christian heritage that is not to be underestimated in the history of the church.

The most significant of the Apostolic Fathers is Ignatius, the bishop of Antioch in Syria. Only a little that is certain has been passed down to us about his life. Origen and Eusebius report that he was the successor of Peter and Euodius as bishop of Antioch.

Malalas recounts that the Christians of Antioch were held responsible for the earthquake that shook the city in A.D. 115. Ignatius was arrested for that and convicted in the same year. He suffered martyrdom in A.D. 116. December 20 is regarded as the day of his death. Even with this uncertainly attested date, however, the date would be around the time of his arrest.[1] Basically all these dates for Ignatius only hold together for certain when the last years

---

1. Downey, *History*, 292–93. Diverging from the general view, Heinrich Kraft suggests that Ignatius's death first happened during the time of Hadrian (A.D. 117–138; Heilmann and Kraft, *Texte der Kirchenväter*, 5.295).

Introduction

of his life coincide with the last years of the reign of Trajan (A.D. 98-117).

When Ignatius was brought as a prisoner to Rome from Syria, he wrote seven letters while under way. From Smyrna he wrote to the Christians in Ephesus, Magnesia, Tralles, and Rome. From Troas he wrote to the communities in Philadelphia and Smyrna and to Polycarp, the bishop of Smyrna. The authenticity of the letters was long disputed. However, today their authenticity is regarded as established due to the findings of famous scholars like Zahn and Lightfoot. There are other letters and some other literary works that are attributed to Ignatius, whose authenticity cannot be established.

The seven letters that are accepted as authentic show us Ignatius as a fearless, passionate witness of the Lord. He possesses a unique, quite bold, and living style that is rich in images, but grammatically is very unbalanced. Therefore, his train of thought is not always logical.[2]

Ignatius's letters are the most significant literary work of the post-apostolic time.[3] They form a valuable source for the order and development of the church's doctrine in the second century. Above all in the research, emphasis is placed on Ignatius's gain with regard to the further development and structure of the monarchic episcopacy and the ecclesial offices. He is also considered the creator of the concept of the catholic church. Further, he was an intransigent

---

2. Bardenhewer, *Geschichte der altkirchlien Literatur*, 1.121-22. "Eine bedeutende, mit wunderbarer Schärfe ausgeprägte Persönlichkeit atmet aus jedem Worte; es lässt sich nichts Individuelleres denken. Dementsprechend ist auch der Stil von höchster Leidenschaft und Formlosigkeit. Es gibt wohl kein Schriftstück jener Zeit, welches in annähernd so souveräner Weise die Sprache vergewaltigte" (Norden, *Die antike Kunstprosa* 2.510-12). Rackl, *Christologie*, 3-4.

3. "Die Ignatianischen Briefe sind mehr, als irgend welche Reliquien des kirchlichen Alterthums bis zu Gregor von Nazianz oder Basilius, Hieronymus oder Augustin hin, der treue Abdruck einer eigenthümlich angelegten und entwickelten Persönlichkeit, hierin wie keine anderen den paulinischen Briefen und nur diesen vergelichbar" (Zahn, *Ignatius von Antiochien*, 400). "They are important today because they contain the earliest reflections of Christian life outside the New Testament" (Grant, *Ignatius*, 12).

Introduction

opponent of all false doctrines and a glowing representative of the ideal martyr. The first steps toward the Hellenization of the gospel likewise become clearly apparent in his letters.[4]

In the current volume, Ignatius's doctrine is now examined under the central themes of the two concepts "faith" and "love." However, one must consider that it is questionable whether Ignatius was a systematic thinker and hence whether one can really speak of his "doctrine." At any rate, he has not left behind a strong theological system. Admittedly, he expresses his insights with enthusiastic commitment to the cause of Jesus Christ, yet his expressions are not always logical and do not always fall within a fixed framework. Nevertheless, we want to set about speaking of his "doctrine." He is one of the first Apostolic Fathers who began a systematic fight against all false doctrines and consequently initiated a first definition of the concept of the faith. Thus he stands at the beginning of dogmatic thought in the post-apostolic time. Seen in this light, his fragmentary statements appear as a kind of whole. The two concepts of faith and love are a pair of words that occur often in Ignatius's letters, and the examination of the pair's contents leads to the root of his theological thought. In what follows, what these concepts mean when interconnected should be examined on the one hand. On the other, one should examine what they contain if one analyzes each of them separately.

Thorough research on Ignatius has gone on for almost a century. To the oldest expositions belong Theodor Zahn, *Ignatius* (1873), J. B. Lightfoot, *The Apostolic Fathers*, Part II (1885), and Eduard von der Goltz, *Ignatius als Christ und Theologe* (1895). These works are still deeply significant today. After their appearance, the research on this field quieted, particularly on the Protestant side. However, the last four decades brought a new boom. Heinrich Schlier published the work *Religionsgeschichtliche Untersuchungen zu den Ignatiusbriefen* in 1929. The work *Gnostiches Gut und Gemeindetradition bei Ignatius* (1940) by Hans-Werner Bartsch is also strongly informed by the perspective of the history-of-religions.[5]

---

4. Riesenfeld, "Reflections," 312.

5. In this work (*Gnostisches Gut*, 6) Bartsch outlines three periods in

Introduction

Peter Meinhold has on several occasions published smaller studies of Ignatius. Hans Freiherr von Campenhausen, the famous Professor of Early Church History, has also treated Ignatius, among others, in his work *Die Idee des Martyriums in der alten Kirche* (2nd ed. 1964). Christian Maurer explores Ignatius's relationship to John in his *Ignatius von Antiochien und das Johannesevangelium* (1949). Theodor Rüsch deals extensively with Ignatius in his study *Die Entstehung der Lehre vom Heiligen Geist* (1952). From Anglophone scholarship, Virginia Corwin's *St. Ignatius and Christianity in Antioch* (1960) should be mentioned as well as Glanville Downey's *A History of Antioch in Syria* (1961), C. C. Richardson's *The Christianity of Ignatius of Antioch* (1935), and T. F. Torrance's *The Doctrine of Grace in the Apostolic Fathers* (1960). M. Rackl treated the christological problem at its most fundamental in the work *Die Christologie des heiligen Ignatius von Antiochien* that already appeared in 1914. Rudolf Bultmann compares the relationship between Ignatius and Paul in his article "Ignatius und Paulus" (*Studia Paulina*, 1953). Werner Bieder, among others, has treated the problem of silence (*Theologische Zeitschrift*, 1956). Apart from these, one finds material about Ignatius in numerous other works and articles as well as in church histories, commentaries (among others, Grant), dogmatic histories, and reference works. The chief works are in German or English; in French, articles especially from the perspective of Catholic research appear.

Die apostolischen Väter, Neubearbeitung der Funkschen Ausgabe von Karl Bihlmeyer (1956) and *Ignatius von Antiochien: Briefe. Erläutert von Gerhard Crone* (1958) underlie this study as editions of the text. The German translation text stems from the publication *Die apostolischen Väter* (1956) by Joseph A. Fischer.

The examination of the concepts of faith and love in Ignatian theology brings us directly to the center around which the

---

Ignatius-research. In the first period, which finds its close in Zahn, the concern was chiefly about the authenticity of the letters. In the next period, in which von der Goltz was decisive, one saw Ignatius in the chain of tradition from Paul and John to the Modalists and Irenaeus. The third period is characterized by the history-of-religions method. Today the age of the history-of-religions school seems also to be past in Ignatian research.

Introduction

dynamic and impulsive thought of Ignatius circles. But it also leads into the problems that appeared in the life of the young church; it shows us the currents that defined the church at the turn of the first century. The statements of the martyr-bishop from Antioch to these contemporary questions do not remain time-bound; they give direction to the future. Even if Ignatius does not number among the actual creators of Christian dogma, he still steers his course through his responses, which are often strongly shaped by his personality, to various questions in this field. In many places, the course that the church will take in the next centuries already becomes apparent in him. Ignatius lived in a time of upheaval. He was a man who knew that he had to lead the way in order to be a sign. An engrossing infiltration into the particularities of his thought will lead to the way in which he subjected himself to this task in detail.

I

Faith and Love as Central Themes of Ignatian Thought

There are a number of concepts that appear again and again in the dynamic and driving thought of Ignatius. Those which emerge most often are the two concepts of *faith* and *love*. They often occur connected with one another. There is no other pair of words in Ignatius's letters that stands in such close connection. In this chapter, then, the focus is on the two concepts that are able to render entirely and completely the whole content of the Christian message.[1]

We find a general definition of these concepts in *Smyrn.* 6.1, "A position should not make anyone proud, for the whole (ὅλον) is faith and love, which nothing surpasses." In this verse Ignatius alerts the recipients of the letter to the temptation that can approach a person in an ecclesiastical office or in a position of trust and to the danger of pride and boasting. Consequently, he points to the foundation of a right faith: in Ignatius's mind proper Christianity is sustained by faith and love. Therefore, an

---

1. An index-like study on the occurrence of the concept of ἀγάπη in Ignatius but also regarding the use of the two concepts of faith and love can be found in Colson, "Agapè," 341–53.

admonition subsequently follows here that was rightly addressed to the lower officeholders, the elders and deacons, and that should have rebuked them for their human weaknesses and their appetite for false fame.[2] This thought is very nearly a plea in the text. Each one must overcome their own "I" and burst the sphere of selfishness in order to infiltrate the central truth of the Christian faith.

The thought that faith and love are the foundation on which each Christian life has to build is not an image that is applied only for rhetorical reasons in Ignatius. He outlines again and again the central significance and basic content of these two concepts in the most varied contexts and in countless places. An example should demonstrate this clearly.

The way that these two concepts comprise the entirety of the Christian faith is emphasized in the following verse in *Eph.* 14.1.

> None of these things escapes you if you direct faith and love, which are the beginning and the end of life, perfectly toward Jesus Christ. Faith is the beginning, love the end. But the two in unity are God. Everything else that belongs to virtue follows from that.

In these words, faith and love are the key to the holiest secrets of the Christian faith. Everything that constitutes the life of a Christian can be extrapolated from these two concepts. If a person is not permeated with faith and love, he remains excluded from God's redemptive and salvific acts. But if a person is taken into these redemptive and salvific acts, he starts out in faith and effects love to the end. The somewhat enigmatic expression, "but the two in unity are God," must mean that God himself is present in the realization of faith and love.[3] Because the Word of God became flesh

---

2. "Office should exalt no one—angels, rulers visible or invisible (cf. Col 1.16, as in *Trall.* 5.2), perhaps some presbyter and deacons?—for nothing is preferable to faith and love (so *Magn.* 1.2; peace, *Eph.* 13.2; Jesus Christ, *Magn.* 7.1; unity, *Pol.* 1.2)" (Grant, *Ignatius*, 119).

3. "None of these matters (related to the harmony, faith, and peace discussed in ch. 13) is hidden (cf. 15.3, 'nothing is hidden from the Lord,' and 19.1, three mysteries hidden from the prince of this age) if faith and love toward Jesus Christ are perfect (perfect faith, *Smyrn.* 10.2; perfect love, 1 John 4.18). Faith is the beginning of (true, Christian) life, while love is its end; this

Faith and Love as Central Themes of Ignatian Thought

in Christ, his will and Spirit can now take up residence in human beings. Faith is the moving power that induces a being from love and in love in the way that a Christian should live.

Other verses document the central meaning of the concepts of faith and love in Ignatius. He writes that he is full of joy because the community in Smyrna is filled with faith and love.[4] He wishes that success may be granted to the Christians in Magnesia for everything that they do in faith and love.[5] He speaks about the unity of faith with love, which nothing surpasses.[6] He calls the much-loved name of the Ephesians, which they have acquired by right nature according to the faith and love in Christ Jesus, welcome in God.[7] He also greets the house of Tavia, whom he desires to remain in both fleshly and spiritual faith and love.[8] Ignatius enshrines the community in Smyrna that is perfect in unmovable faith, as if nailed to the cross of the Lord Jesus Christ with flesh and spirit, and is established in love in Christ's blood.[9] "If you believe in love..."[10]—this clause also shows the close connection, the

---

is common Christian doctrine (Bauer, [*Briefe*,] p. 213). When faith is united with love, God is present; compare 1 John 4.8: 'he who does not love does not know God; for God is love' (see Nygren, *Agape and Eros*, 261). Everything else leading to 'nobility of character' (*kalokagathia*; in Philo but here only in early Christian literature) is consequent upon faith and love" (Grant, *Ignatius*, 44–45).

4. *Smyrn.* inscr.

5. *Magn.* 13.1.

6. *Magn.* 1.2.

7. *Eph.* 1.1. A probable connection can be found here with the thought in the letter to the Ephesians by Paul (5:2): "And walk in love just as Christ loved us and gave himself for us as an offering and sacrifice" (Grant, *Ignatius*, 31).

8. *Smyrn.* 13.1.

9. *Smyrn.* 1.1. Vial emphasizes Ignatius's faith in Jesus: "Pour Ignace, le seul vivant est celui qui croit en Jésus. Cette foi le hante et lui fait clamer violemment aux chrétiens: 'En dehors de Lui que rien n'ait de valeur pour vous'; 'soyez sourds quand on vous parle d'autre chose que de Jésus-Christ'" (*Ignace d'Antioche*, 76).

10. *Phld.* 9.2. Prior to this, Ignatius has referred to Christ as the door to the Father, through which the Patriarchs and Prophets entered. "All together—Old Testament and gospel— are good (related to salvation) if Christians combine faith with love" (Grant, *Ignatius*, 107).

Faith and Love in Ignatius of Antioch

inseparability of faith and love in Ignatius. Even a scholar such as Seeberg, who thinks that three main concepts in Ignatian theology can be presented, that is, faith, love, and hope, still concludes that the first two concepts comprise the entire content of the Christian life in themselves.[11]

What does Ignatius understand by faith as "the beginning" of the Christian life and love as its "end?" At this point it must be remembered that Ignatius lived in an age in which the basic notions of the Christian message were still quite clear and plainly in consciousness for believers. The new faith was chiefly a faith in Jesus Christ, who suffered, died, and was raised for us. Christianity radically differentiated itself through this conviction from other contemporaneous religions. Judaism could not acknowledge Jesus as the Son of God and thus also could not grasp that his blood is the atonement for humanity's sins. Christianity really had no common foundation with gentile religions, since it advocated a completely new and other vision of the relationship between a person and God. The message of Christ and his work, the gospel of the cross and resurrection, formed the core of Christian faith. Likewise, it is always evident in another context that, with the concept of faith, Ignatius is thinking of this central event and considers it the foundation of the Christian faith.[12] This faith is not "dead"; it is

---

11. "Wir reden zweitens von der Bestimmung des Christenlebens als Glaube, Liebe, Hoffnung, oder auch nur Glaube und Liebe" (Seeberg, *Lehrbuch*, 183, 185).

12. Many scholars emphasize the central position of Christ in Ignatius's conception of faith. "Im Mittelpunkt steht Jesus Christus. Seine Gott darstellende und offenbarende menschliche Person und sein Durchdringen durch den Tod zum Leben sind nicht nur Offenbarung der Gottesliebe und ethisches Vorbild, sondern für die ganze Menschheit Verbürgerung der Erfassung Gottes in ihm, des ewigen in der Zeit, der Hoffnung ewigen Lebens in seinem Tode" (von der Goltz, *Ignatius*, 86). "Faith is implicit trust in Christ, absolute obedience to him and to his manner of life. It includes the firm conviction that Christ is God become man, and that he has revealed to men the character of the Father. Faith is the assurance that Christ is the bringer of life, it is the abiding hope in the resurrection and unwavering personal confidence in the indwelling presence of the Lord, whom after death the believer will meet in that life of communion with Him, which is life indeed" (Richardson, *Christianity*, 6). "Faith is the response of man to what God has already done. It

Faith and Love as Central Themes of Ignatian Thought

not the acceptance of historical facts as true. Rather the good fight of faith in the community and a truly living and inner trust in the Lord are meant.[13] Christian spirituality signifies the same thing as Christian faith in Ignatius; it means that which Paul calls "being in Christ."[14]

What then does ἀγάπη mean when used by Ignatius in this context? According to Richardson, ἀγάπη in Ignatius is a lifestyle permeated by brotherly love.[15] The understanding of this concept in Ignatius is probably captured correctly with this definition. Love determines the manner and way in which the faithful lead their daily life. With it, they have reached an "end." There is no way to a further perfection. The Christian life, as it ought to be, is a life permeated by love. The law of love is binding for their overall conduct. It prohibits everything evil toward the neighbor, and it calls to service, humility, and selflessness.

Love thus demonstrates itself in daily life; it proves itself in whether a person has the right disposition and the right faith. "No one who professes faith sins, and the one who possesses love does not hate. One knows the tree by its fruit. Thus those who profess to be Christ's disciples will become apparent by their actions. For it does not come down to the profession but whether one is found in the power of faith at the end" (*Eph.* 14.2). With this line of thought, Ignatius aligns himself with New Testament tradition. Synoptic and Johannine transmissions thus appear side by side for him.[16] "Either plant a good tree so there will be good fruit, or plant a rotten tree, so there will be rotten fruit. For one recognizes the tree by its fruit" (Matt 12:33). Thus Jesus preached, and Ignatius has adopted these thoughts verbatim. According to Matt 24:13, the one who is blessed is the one who perseveres in temptations to the

---

wells up in man because God has acted in the death and resurrection of Jesus Christ" (Corwin, *St. Ignatius*, 238).

13. Faith in Ignatius concerns a "vital personal devotion to the Lord Jesus Christ" (Richardson, *Christianity*, 10).

14. Rüsch, *Entstehung*, 63–64.

15. Richardson, *Christianity*, 10.

16. Grant, *Ignatius*, 45.

Faith and Love in Ignatius of Antioch

end when love is cooled in many. John bears witness to the love of God for the world (John 3:16) when he says, "Whoever is born of God does not sin" (1 John 5:18). Ignatius now unites these different lines of thought to one another. He has a kind of worldview in which Synoptic and Johannine traditions are found, and he has connected them with one another. A believer cannot sin. A genuine lover cannot hate. A good tree brings good fruit, and an evil tree evil fruit. That is the simple and unambiguous line of Ignatius's ethics. A genuine love cannot remain hidden. It ceaselessly makes its presence felt. Hence the lack of the fruits of the Spirit is a gauge that shows that love is only in words and not in deeds. Such a love, however, is not from God.

The unity of faith and love is indicated in some of Ignatius's expressions in which these two concepts are juxtaposed and then interpreted. "Your faith is your guide upward; love is the way that leads up to God" (*Eph.* 9.1). Faith and love in this verse are depicted as ways that lead up to God. The goal is the same with both. Peter Meinhold has suggested that Ignatius has found a gnostic expression for believers in this verse in *Ephesians*. However, he emphasizes that there is a difference between this and other points of contact, which differentiate Ignatius from Gnosticism.[17] Schlier compared *Eph.* 9.1 with the Manichaean *Acta Archelai*.[18] However, it seems difficult to me to see a connection here. There are indeed terminological similarities when viewed textually (ultimately it is not really surprising that similar forms of expression are found in a time of active religious life), but a large difference exists. Not only in Christianity but also in many other religions, the search for God is depicted as an upward-quest—a search for that which is above and not for that which is on earth. Hence, it is difficult to compare or to draw conclusions because the same term can have a different meaning in various religions.

Yet again to Ignatius. His admonition, "Therefore, take up gentleness and renew yourselves in faith, which is the flesh of the Lord, and in love, which is the blood of Jesus Christ" (*Trall.* 8.1)

17. Meinhold, "Ethik," 53.
18. Schlier, *Religionsgeschichtliche Untersuchungen*, 110.

remains somewhat unclear and ambiguous. The comparison appears rather surprising.[19] What does Ignatius mean by it? Does it consist in a reference to the Lord's Supper and should the bread and the wine symbolize Christ's body and blood as well as faith and love?[20] Lietzmann sees here a clear connection with thoughts on the Lord's Supper and also with the Johannine world and with love.[21] Ignatius probably wants to express the following: as flesh is the formative part and the circulation of blood is the energizing part in bodies, so also both faith and love act as the necessary parts for the Christian life. Each has its own task but one cannot exist without the other. One cannot think of either for its own sake. They first collectively form an entirety that is irreplaceable.

Ignatius's advice follows the old image of the *militia Christi*. "Let your baptism remain as weaponry, faith as a helmet, love as a spear, patience as armor" (*Pol.* 6.2). Ignatius may have known the image already from the Old Testament ("He put on righteousness as a breastplate and the helmet of salvation on his head"; Isa 59:17). However, it is more probable that Ignatius takes over the image from Eph 6:13–17, where the passage speaks about the entire armor of God, about the breastplate of righteousness, about the helmet of salvation, and about the sword of the Spirit. The images that are used in Ignatius and in Ephesians do not correspond exactly. The same Christian virtues are not represented through the weapons. However, the purpose is the same, namely, to show that as earthly weapons find their use in earthly warfare, so the weapons of the Spirit are used in the same way in spiritual warfare.

When we speak about faith and love, we thus name two of the chief concepts of Christian faith. However, almost no one except for Ignatius moves them, connected with one another, into the central point of their entire thought like this. This man, who had

---

19. Grant, *Ignatius*, 77.

20. "The reference is only indirectly to the eucharist. The eucharistic bread and wine, while representing the flesh and blood of Christ, represent also faith and love. Faith is the flesh, the substance of the Christian life; love is the blood, the energy coursing through its veins and arteries" (Lightfoot, *Apostolic Fathers*, 2.2.171).

21. Lietzmann, *Geschichte*, 1.256.

death in view, doubtless wanted to express clearly what appeared to him to be the most important thing. Faith and love became for him the words in which the entire content of Christian faith, *summa totius theologiae*, could be outlined. These two words grasp the beginning and the end of life's way and everything that lies between. This definition is very general. One could almost consider it shallow. Still, it should express that both faith as well as love, dogmatics and also ethics, justification and salvation, are indivisibly connected with one another. However, with the assessment that both faith and love lead upward, to God, Ignatius differentiates himself from a man like Luther. According to the latter, love leads to the neighbor, below, in the middle of daily life, to service of the other. Yet this view is also found in Ignatius, even if in another context. He emphasizes that the good fruits of the Spirit are essential and thereby represents the same thing.

When Ignatius juxtaposes faith and love, he wants to create a connection between faith and the new life in love. To establish a balance between these two is surely one of the basic problems of the Christian faith! If faith is emphasized too much, the danger threatens that it falls into a kind of empty space and withers. Its training ground, daily Christian life, is isolated from it. It remains without the possibility to bring fruit. By contrast, when the main emphasis lies on new life, love, and ethical perfection, the Christian faith turns into morality. The inner life and the streams of living water are then desiccated. In Ignatian thought, we can see a first, noteworthy attempt to link faith and life firmly to one another in love to produce a balance between them. Pauline faith and Johannine love belong indissolubly to living Christianity. They cannot be separated from one another.

If Ignatius speaks about faith and love as he speaks about this unity, much is intended in these two concepts that is not expressly said. Ignatius knows that he is in agreement with New Testament tradition. However, these two concepts also occur alone and in different settings within his letters. Therefore, they belong to one another, but they still have a unique imprint, a specific character for the given situation in the overall context. The following chapters are now devoted to the study of the respective contents of faith and love.

2

Faith

1. Right Belief

The time of early Christianity was, more than other times in church history, a time of struggle and great controversies. The young church was still in a genuine sense *ecclesia militans*. The authorities regarded Christians with the greatest mistrust, persecutions were nothing unusual, even the bias of the local area was often hostile against Christians. In addition, an inner crisis arose in the church itself. Repeatedly and on ever new fronts questions sprang up: What is the right doctrine that is binding for all? What is the ground on which all are able to build? Paul already lamented divisions in the community of Corinth (1 Cor 1:10–17) and condemned people who preferred the "basic powers" (elements) of the world and did not place their trust in Jesus Christ (Col 2:20). Both letters to Timothy and the letter to Titus oppose Jewish-gnostic false teachings; they advise members of the community to avoid contact with adherents of such false teachings. 2 Peter, Jude, and two of John's letters (1 and 2 John) express similar warnings.[1]

---

1. Hutten, *Glaubenswelt*, 11. Hutten produces a short survey of the history of sectarianism, but in doing so he has not considered the time of the

Faith

This struggle for right belief, and this exchange with emerging false teachers was pursued in the post-apostolic time. Ignatius took part in it with burning zeal for the Lord's cause. Although he was first of all a passionate witness for the faith, who considered martyrdom the only goal of the Christian life worth striving for and who wanted to fulfill this goal as quickly as possible, he still turned out to be a far-sighted church leader. He was clear that not just any worldview could find its way into Christian doctrine, which is the foundation of the church. A community needs clear and unambiguous standards—standards that agree with the doctrine of their founder, Jesus Christ.

In his *Ecclesiastical History* (3.36), Eusebius already indicates how Ignatius always admonished in order to shelter from emerging false teachers and how he always emphasized that it is important to adhere to apostolic heritage. His entire literary activity (his letters) serves this purpose. In a similar way, both older and more recent scholarship see the principal significance of Ignatius in this struggle against invading false teachers.[2]

Ignatius cautions against sectarianism and schism in several places. He urges the Christians to stay far away from them and to avoid them (μερισμοὺς φεύγετε; *Smryn.* 7.2; *Phld.* 7.2). He praises the Ephesians because no false doctrine has arisen among them (οὐδεμία αἵρεσις; *Eph.* 6.1). However, where schism and wrath prevail, there God does not dwell (*Phld.* 8.1). Believers should only use Christian food and avoid false teachers, who are foreign weeds

---

Apostolic Fathers. Goppelt determines that no corresponding terminology for false teaching developed at the end of the apostolic time (*Die apostolische und nachapostolische Zeit*, 113). In general, Old Testament-Jewish idioms were applied in compounds with ψευδ- and ἑτερο-. In the Pastoral Epistles the word αἱρετικὸς ἄνθρωπος occasionally appears (Titus 3:10).

2. "Die bedeutsameren theologischen Äusserungen des Ignatius sind durch den Gegensatz der damals in Kleinasien Eingang suchenden Häresie hervorgerufen. Der schlechten, schliesslich vom Teufel stammenden Lehre, durch welche jene Irrlehrer den wahren Glauben und damit die Kirche verderben (*Eph.* 9; 16; 17), stellt er die wahre Gotteserkenntnis gegenüber..." (Zahn, *Ignatius von Antiochien*, 454). "Im Ketzerkampf des 2. Jahrhunderts vor Justin gilt als wichtigster und erfolgreichster Vertreter der Kirchenlehre Ignatius, der Martyrer von Antiochien" (Bauer, *Rechtgläubigkeit und Ketzerei*, 65).

(*Trall.* 6.1). They should eschew evil weeds who are not planted by the Father and were not cultivated by Jesus Christ (*Phld.* 3.1). Believers should also not be shaken by those who are trustworthy on the face of it and still are aberrant teachers (ἑτεροδιδασκαλοῦντες; *Pol.* 3.1).

A number of biblical images and comparisons are found in these warnings. Isaiah already related the vineyard and its cultivation (Isa 5). Jesus speaks about the planting that the Heavenly Father did not plant and that should be exterminated (Matt 15:13). The discourse about the incompatibility of hate and exasperation, on the one hand, and Christian love that has God's promise, on the other, suggests Johannine influence. Different images are fitted into each other in the following. "So, now, as children of the light of truth, flee schism and wicked doctrine. But where the shepherd is, follow there as sheep. For many wolves, who pretend to be trustworthy, snatch away God's people through wicked pleasure" (*Phld.* 2.1). The image of the shepherd and the sheep appears chiefly in the Bible (Matt 7:15; 10:16; Luke 10:3). The danger to which Ignatius alludes with this comparison does not threaten only from the outside like an attacking and powerful predator but also from the inside in insidious deception, full of guile and cunning.

The designations for "false doctrine" that Ignatius uses most frequently are μερισμός and αἵρεσις. The terms κακοδιδασκαλία and κακὴ διδασκαλία occur as well. The latter term is found in *Eph.* 16 with the meaning "wicked doctrine." "Do not be deceived, my brothers. Those who corrupt households will not inherit the kingdom of God. If then those who do these things according to the flesh die, how much more the one who corrupts the faith of God for which Jesus was crucified by wicked doctrine" (*Eph.* 16.1–2). As a temple is profaned through misuse, so is the faith corrupted through wicked teaching according to Ignatius (cf. Rom 2:22; 1 Cor 6:9; Eph 5:5; Matt 24:4). The comparison with God's house, the center of the community, emphasizes the crucial meaning of doctrine for the faithful. If the doctrine is wrong, everything falters. As the holiness of the church building must be sacrosanct, so also must the doctrine be the foundation of the faith.

Faith

A further term for sectarianism is found in the letter to the community in Philadelphia. "Do not be deceived, my brothers. If someone follows a schismatic (σχίζοντι<σχίζων<σχίζειν), he does not inherit the kingdom of God. If someone walks in foreign doctrine (ἐν ἀλλοτρίᾳ γνώμῃ), he does not agree with (Christ's) passion" (*Phld.* 3.3). Here Ignatius uses a word (σχίζειν) that means to scatter, diverge, and disintegrate (cf. schizophrenia).

In this designation for false doctrine, the same thought comes to expression as in the later-used designation "sect" (Lat. *sectum*—cut off, fragmented). Sectarianism always means the cutting off of a part from a whole, a divergence, a going astray, and a digression on unfamiliar paths. Unity is destroyed, and fragmentation and ruin take its place.

It is amazing that Ignatius does not say a word about pagan cults, movements, and concepts of belief in the Hellenistic period.[3] Perhaps he considered Christians' hostile stance against them so natural that a closer examination of them was no longer necessary. Instead, he attaches even more value to turning foreign thoughts that want to gain a foothold inside Christianity away in time.

The two ways that Ignatius particularly opposes in his struggle against false doctrine are Judaism and docetism. He spots these two ways that diverge from right doctrine, for example, among Christians in Syria. For the so-called Judaizers, to adhere to Judaism was seen as a prerequisite for Christian faith. These people would not understand that the new age had finally begun with Christ. Furthermore, they considered the law of Moses compulsory for Christians with its numerous commands and prohibitions. The other way, the docetists, were particularly attracted to gnostic doctrine. However, under gnostic influence the Christian doctrine unexpectedly receives an essentially alien interpretation.[4]

Opinion is now divided in scholarship about whether Ignatius's allegations concern two different groups of opponents, i.e., whether there is another gnostically oriented group besides the Judaizers, or whether it concerns the same people both times.

---

3. Riesenfeld, "Reflections," 313.
4. Lightfoot, *Apostolic Fathers*, 2.2.124.

Faith and Love in Ignatius of Antioch

According to Molland, the impression is never aroused as if Ignatius has fought against two different groups. Thus he reproaches the same opponents as both Judaism and docetism. Molland sees evidence in *Magn.* 8–11 that both of these ways that diverge from right doctrine are principally one.[5] This view has been the *communis opinio* since the seventies and eighties of the previous century, since the time of Theodor Zahn and Lightfoot. However, according to Hans-Werner Bartsch, it concerns two different groups—a group of Judaizaers and one of docetists.[6] Joseph A. Fischer likewise considered Molland's claims to lack adequate foundation.[7]

A final decision for one or the other of the views is not possible due to the available material. Indeed, evidence can be cited for both points of view, but it is, in any case, not of persuasive cogency for one view or the other. The question must therefore be left open. It can only be determined that Ignatius fights against two ways as far as the false teachers are concerned, namely, against Judaism and docetism; however, whether these are represented by one and the same group of people remains undecided.

Ignatius writes about Judaism:

> There is no place for confessing Jesus Christ and for living in a Jewish manner. For Christianity has not believed in Judaism but rather Judaism in Christianity, to which every tongue that believes in God has been gathered (*Magn.* 10.3).

Ignatius invokes here the historical development that corresponds to God's salvific designs. Judaism was indeed there in the first place. Yet God's revelation strove in a clearly recognizable fashion to its completion, finally transformed the promise into fulfillment, and began once and for all the new aeon—the time of the new faith. If a person who intends to be a Christian adheres to the Jewish faith of the law, they proceed to a way that leads backwards in the wrong direction. The way from Judaism to Christianity is

---

5. Molland, "Heretics," 3–4.
6. Bartsch, *Gnostische Gut*, 34–39.
7. Fischer, *Die apostolischen Väter*, 119n.13.

Faith

natural; it corresponds to God's purpose. By contrast, the reverse situation is an absurdity. However, Ignatius must admit that this way is nevertheless repeatedly used. Adherents of Judaism also confess Christ as their Lord, but they show by their return under the yoke of the law that they have not yet really grasped the message of the new faith. For did not Paul, an apostle of Jesus Christ, declare, "Christ has set us free for freedom! Stand firm, then, and do not let yourself be caught again in the slavish yoke" (Gal 5:1)? Whether Ignatius knew this Pauline expression is not certain. However, the matter about which the apostle speaks also belongs to the most important things for him, and he always opposes the false teachers expressly for this in his struggle. Thus, in another place in the same letter he says, "If we live until now according to Judaism, we confess that we have not received grace" (*Magn.* 8.1). In this verse, Ignatius expresses clearly that Christianity is rather a *religion of grace*, unlike Judaism where the thought of merit plays a great role and is a religion of the law.

The legalism of Jewish adherents expresses itself clearly in the strict obedience of the Sabbath command. Those who arrive at faith in Christ and set their hope on him alone no longer keep Sabbath but celebrate the day of the Lord instead. On this day, "our life was also raised through him and his death" (*Magn.* 9.1). It is now necessary to turn toward the new leaven, i.e., toward Jesus Christ (*Magn.* 10.2). Whoever has received grace and Christ as teacher cannot live in a Jewish manner. For them, it has become Sunday, and the Sabbath has ended.[8]

In the context of the Sabbath question, the relationship of Ignatius to the Old Testament is problematic. It involves a verse in Ignatius's letter to the community in Magnesia. He writes here in the beginning of chapter 9 that the prophets already had expected Jesus as teacher and were even his disciples in the Spirit. They had already lived according to the Lord's Day rather than according to the Sabbath. Various views are represented in the research regarding the significance of this verse. According to Einar Molland, older scholars like Zahn, Lightfoot, and Lelong considered

---

8. Seeberg, *Anfänge*, 232.

it quite improbable that Ignatius could have written that the Old Testament prophets kept Sunday in the place of the Sabbath. They hold the view that Ignatius speaks about Jews who are converted to Christianity. Scholars today are of a different mind. Bauer states that an author who also said that the prophets "lived according to Jesus" cannot now suddenly speak about converted Jews. However, when Bauer, following Lightfoot, supposes that the words μηκέτι σαββατίζοντες, ἀλλά expresses a conversion from old to new, that is likewise a quite improbable thought in the context of the prophets. These words are rather to be understood in the following way: the prophets wanted to protest against their surroundings in which they had grown up. They believed in the coming of the Lord and, before his incarnation, already lived "according to the day of the Lord"—thus is the term. Molland considers these terms in *Magn.* 9.1, σαββατίζειν and κατὰ κυριακὴν ζῆν, to be symbolic expressions that mean roughly the same thing as κατὰ Ἰουδαϊσμὸν ζῆν and κατὰ Χριστιανισμὸν ζῆν in *Magn.* 8.1 and 10.1. Based on this, he suggests that Ignatius wants to express that the prophets already had lived in the Christian faith and no longer in the Jewish faith.[9]

This latter solution is probably the most reasonable. According to this, Ignatius considers the prophets a sort of "ancient Christians," who have already obtained in advance the gift of salvation that Christ first brought to humanity. Ignatius wanted the celebration of Sunday by the prophets to be interpreted, probably symbolically, as an anticipation that should bring its expectation of salvation to expression. In his mind, the prophets were already disciples in the Spirit (τῷ πνεύματι; *Magn.* 9.2). Precisely this expression, "in the Spirit," demonstrates that Ignatius has understood the life of the prophets as a time of expectation that already included the desiderated gift of salvation for themselves, however.

Ignatius refers to the prophets at various times in his letters (*Smyrn.* 5.1; 7.2). However, it is striking that his letters do not provide any clues from which one might determine on which verses

---

9. Molland, "Heretics," 3–4.

Faith

in Scripture he is building his argumentation.[10] It is likely that he considers that type of reference so irrelevant that any explanation along this line was unnecessary in his view. There were sufficient things that were weightier for him relating to Christian faith. That is understandable if one considers that Ignatius composed his letters in the face of death.

Although a biblical canon in the contemporary sense was not yet assembled, Ignatius has already had a certain conception of it. In his view, Moses, the Prophets, and the Gospel form the core. He would certainly have also agreed with the Lutheran principle that all students and teachers are to be assessed based on these. Virginia Corwin has indicated that a similarly distinguished significance is ascribed to the Prophets and their prophecy at certain places in the documents from the Dead Sea (*Jubilees*; *Damascus Document*; *Habakkuk Commentary*).[11] However, no evidence can be adduced that Ignatius may have known these sources. It can be presumed as highly likely that great emphasis was laid on the significance of the prophets in the environment in which Ignatius lived. Accordingly, it is then understandable that Ignatius expressly indicates their particular position.

It is noteworthy in this context that direct references to the Old Testament are otherwise almost completely missing in Ignatius.[12] He was certainly not a Jew or Jewish proselyte[13]—that is expressed clearly in his thoughts. A Jew would not have selected a Latin name. According to Riesenfeld, the images and metaphors in his letters are largely Hellenistic in their content and form.[14] As a consequence, this suggests that Ignatius was a converted gentile or possibly even a third-generation Christian.

---

10. Rackl, *Christologie*, 128.

11. Corwin, *St. Ignatius*, 62.

12. Isaiah 5:26 is referred to in *Smyrn.* 1.2. *Trallians* 8.2 may contain a reference to Isa 52:5. Psalm 32:9 (LXX) forms the background of *Eph.* 15.1. Echoes of *Wis.* 7:29–30 and 18:14 can be found in *Eph.* 14. See Grant, *Ignatius*, 56–57.

13. Riesenfeld, "Reflections," 312.

14. Ibid., 317.

Faith and Love in Ignatius of Antioch

In summary, it can now be said that the criticism that Ignatius practiced a Jewishly oriented Christianity is not very rigorous. The same applies when he polemicizes against Judaism. Grant concludes from this that the border between the church and synagogue was not clearly defined and the division was viewed as insurmountable.[15]

In Meinhold's view, the main difference between Ignatius and his opponents lies in the perception of how the Old Testament should be interpreted. For Ignatius's opponents, Judaism forms the historically constituted precursor to Christianity with its chief forms of life that are anchored in the law that therefore remains binding even for Christians. Against this, the Jewish faith constitutes the historical preparation of the Christian faith for Ignatius. However, Jewish faith is overcome once and for all, not only in principle, but also with regard to practical performance, so that "Christianity" appears as the completion of designed attempts that were only hidden in Judaism.[16] It is noteworthy that Ignatius is the first to speak of Christianity (Χριστιανισμός) and clearly refers to the difference with Judaism by this.[17]

In the struggle against docetism, Christ, his earthly life, his birth, his suffering, and his resurrection are at stake.[18] Ignatius does not fight alone on this front—these questions would be hotly disputed for a century. What then is Ignatius specifically on about?

The central place of Jesus Christ is characteristic of his theology. Indeed, God also occupies a central place—an indication of this is simply the fact that the word occurs in the letter 175 times. Hence, Rackl takes this notion christocentrically, a designation that obviously does justice to this theology.[19] Still, the person of the

---

15. Grant, *Ignatius*, 97.

16. Meinhold, "Schweigende Bischöfe," 481.

17. "Von 'Christentum' (Χριστιανισμός) redet zuerst Ignatius von Antiochien, und zwar indem er es als religiöse Haltung vom 'Judentum' unterscheidet, wobei in beiden Fällen zugleich die hinter den religiösen Lebenshaltungen stehenden und für sie massgebenden Glaubensnormen gemeint sind (*Magn.* 10, 1–3)" (Wolf, "Das Wort Christentum," 1696).

18. Lightfoot, *Apostolic Fathers*, 2.2.173.

19. Rackl, *Christologie*, 227.

Faith

Redeemer is particularly emphasized by Ignatius.[20] That is because Ignatius ascribes foundational value to soteriology, that is, to the redemptive work of Jesus Christ. "Let no one be deceived! Even the heavenly powers, the glory of angels, and the visible and invisible leaders—judgment comes over them if they do not believe in the blood of Christ" (*Smyrn.* 6.1). One could suppose Johannine influence here ("the blood of Jesus Christ purifies us from all sins" [1 John 1:7]), but Pauline thoughts could also have been operating (cf. Rom 3:25; 5:9; Eph 1:7; 2:13; Col 1:20). In another place, Ignatius compares the cross of Christ with a lever with which the faithful are pulled upward like stones to the Father's temple (*Eph.* 9.1). Christ is thus the Redeemer who gives reconciliation through his blood to all who believe in him. The maladjusted relationship of the person with God is readjusted through Jesus's death.

But on the docetic understanding, Jesus is a divine entity with a mock body. His suffering was thus only apparent; his death was a sham for those gathered around the cross. There are all kinds of nuances in this Christology, which has been appropriated by Gnosticism. However, the notion is common to all that a heavenly, invisible Christ who is not susceptible to suffering must be differentiated from a lower, earthly Christ. The heavenly Christ is hidden in the earthly Christ and is not really flesh and blood.[21] According to docetic thinking, the redeemer of humanity cannot be apprehended by human ways.[22] This direction thus denies the central Christian truth: in order to bring redemption to sinful humanity, Christ must not only be true God but also true human.

The original time and place of the docetic false teaching cannot be precisely determined. Bousset considers Syria and Asia Minor its home.[23] Places can already be found in the Pauline letters in which the unique place of Christ as true human and true God is emphasized, possibly already in opposition to docetic ways of

---

20. Rüsch, *Entstehung*, 49. "The centre of Ignatius's thinking was Christ" (Kelly, *Early Christian Doctrines*, 92).

21. Kelly, *Early Christian Doctrines*, 142.

22. Nygren, *Den kristna kärlekstanken*, 2.120.

23. Bousset, *Kyrios Christos*, 159.

thinking (Col 1:20; 2:8–10; 1 Tim 2:5; 6:20). The polemic against gnostic false teaching shows itself particularly clearly in the Johannine letters, particularly in 1 John 4:1–3 (4:2: By this you should recognize the Spirit of God: every spirit that confesses that Jesus Christ has come in the flesh is from God) and in 2 John 7. Rackl does not want to go that far. In his view, Ignatius would have been the first to fight docetism as an independent phenomenon.[24] In general, however, scholars see in these words John's challenge to gnostic false teaching. The false teachers have made a merely spiritual being out of Christ. They deny his incarnation.[25]

Ignatius expressed the central idea of his christological thought in *Trallians*.

> Therefore, be deaf when someone speaks to you without Jesus Christ, who stems from the family of David, from Mary, who was truly born, both ate and drank, was truly persecuted under Pontius Pilate, was truly crucified, and died before the eyes of those who are in heaven, on earth, and under the earth (*Trall.* 9.1).

As in the Apostles' Creed, Ignatius refers to Jesus's historical background by naming the proconsul Pontius Pilate, in whose time all these things transpired. The history of Jesus Christ is thus not concerned with some timeless myth of such a kind as is found chiefly in the Hellenistic realm. Ignatius emphasizes exactly the opposite of this kind of ideological notion by explicitly referring to Jesus as a historical personality. Everything that is recounted of him is historical reality: and the Word became flesh and dwelled among us (John 1:14). Ignatius wants to underline this Johannine way of thinking and this reality of the incarnation.

The docetists were also clear in their mind that Christianity cannot be taught without Christ occupying a fitting place in the teaching system. "They mix Jesus Christ and pretend to be trustworthy, as if handing a deadly gift with honeyed-wine that the ignorant gladly accept with evil pleasure. It is their death" (*Trall.*

---

24. Rackl, *Christologie*, 96, 98.
25. Cf. Hauck, *Briefe des Jakobus*, 141; Lauha, *Katoliset kirjeet*, 106.

Faith

6.2). These false teachers bring a wrong image of Christ that is not always easy to differentiate from the right image. They take Christ into their doctrine only outwardly and only apparently.[26]

Right belief thus depends on the confession of Christ's true humanity. At the time of Ignatius, this appeared to be much more difficult than belief in his divinity. For this reason, Ignatius leaves plenty of space in his letters for warnings about the docetists. In various places, he speaks about Christ's birth and origin "according to the flesh." Jesus stems from David's seed (*Rom.* 7.3; *Eph.* 20.2), from David's family according to the flesh, truly born of a virgin (*Smyrn.* 1.1), from David's family and from Mary (*Trall.* 9.1). He expressly emphasizes, "For our God, Jesus the Christ, was carried in Mary's womb, from David's seed and also from the Holy Spirit according to God's plan" (*Eph.* 18.2). Nothing that is connected with Jesus's birth is a random coincidence of fate, even his descent from an earthly family. Rather, all these things belong to the great and encompassing salvific plan of God—to his "economy." In Judaism, as generally in the Semitic world, great value was placed upon family tradition. For this reason, both the New Testament authors and later Christian writers have also emphasized the significance of Jesus's family tree and his descent from David.[27]

According to Ignatius, the life of Jesus was the life of a normal person. He "ate and drank" (*Trall.* 9.1) because, like any person, he did not manage without nourishment. He was "truly crucified for us in the flesh under Pontius Pilate and Herod the Tetrarch" (*Smyrn.* 1.2). "Yet the gospel has something special: the arrival of the redeemer, our Lord Jesus Christ, his suffering, and resurrection" (*Phld.* 9.2). "He truly suffered as he also was truly raised. He

---

26. Meinhold, "Schweigende Bischöfe," 476; Andrén, *Apostoliska fäderna*, 80.

27. "As Bauer points out, in the second century Mary was usually regarded as descended from David—not only in apocryphal literature such as the Protoevangelium and 3 Corinthians 5, but also by Justin, Tatian, Irenaeus, and Clement. Presumably the genealogies in Matthew 1:2–16 and Luke 3:23–38 were regarded as genealogies of Mary, not of Joseph (whom Ignatius never mentions)" (Grant, *Ignatius*, 48).

Faith and Love in Ignatius of Antioch

did not suffer in appearance, as some unbelievers say" (*Smyrn.* 2; cf. *Trall.* 9.2; 10).

Ignatius's words are a conscious, emphatic protest against docetic thoughts. He thus wants to emphasize that the earthly existence of Christ was a real life that was subject to the laws of historical conditions of existence.[28] Even after his resurrection he demonstrated his corporeal form. "And when he came to Peter and his companions, he said to them, 'Touch me, feel me and see that I am not a bodiless demon.' And immediately they touched him and believed because they came into close connection with his flesh and spirit" (*Smyrn.* 3.2). Lightfoot pointed to the fact that the word that is used in this context (κραθέντες) expresses the greatest possible nearness in companionship.[29] The meal with the disciples shows that even after the Easter event Jesus was still found in a concrete, corporeal form. "But after the resurrection he ate and drank with them as a corporeal being, while he was also spiritually united with the Father" (*Smyrn.* 3.3).

On Ignatius's view, right belief is also a belief in Christ as a true human being who has the same earthly origin as everyone of us and whose birth occurred exactly as with human children before his own birth, who lived according to the same laws of life as other people and whose course of life was also closely bound to history like all people. He was no mere appearance, not only a spirit, but rather flesh and blood. If that is impugned, the foundation of Christian faith is denied. Christ had to stand under the laws to which human life is bound. Otherwise, a redemption of humanity was not possible. The doctrine of redemption represented by Anselm is embedded embryonically in this thought. *Satisfactio*

---

28. The historicity is stressed in many ways according to Virginia Corwin. "When he says that the birth, the suffering, the crucifixion 'truly' happened, he is trying to affirm the fact that they occurred on the ordinary scene of human life—are what we would call historical events. If we had any reason for believing he knew a creed, we might admit that reference to the crucifixion under Pontius Pilate is a creedal phrase; but when he goes on to add 'and in the reign of Herod the Tetrarch' we must conclude that he does this to offer more evidence of the inescapable reality of the fact" (*St. Ignatius*, 114).

29. Lightfoot, *Apostolic Fathers*, 2.2.297.

requires that the redeemer is a true human being because no one else can atone for our disobedience.

The image of the redeemer in Ignatius is concrete and living. It can be assumed that stories about Jesus were orally passed down even in his time. This passing down certainly occurred already in the second or third generation, but it was yet still so living that, through it, one could visualize the master wandering on earth. It appears as if Ignatius has so firmly emphasized the true humanity of Jesus based precisely on these stories. Ignatius constitutes a passing down as the third bishop of Antioch. His predecessors in this office should have been Peter and Euodius. If this is right, a special maintenance of Jesus-tradition probably stood in close connection with this office. That would have helped to strengthen Ignatius's conviction with regard to the importance of belief in the historical Jesus.

The events of Jesus's birth and death are peculiarly presented in *Eph.* 19. These events are here described as "loudly crying mysteries" that remained hidden from the ruler of this world. They were completed in God's silence but revealed themselves to the aeons as a radiant star.[30] The notion of the devil's deception, of the deception of the powers of hell, is probably encountered for the first time in Christian literature in this verse by Ignatius.[31] A favorite theme of later patristics is here.[32] This concept emerges in, among others, Origen and Gregory of Nyssa. Schlier supposes an extra-Christian

---

30. "1And the virginity of Mary and her giving birth were hidden from the ruler of this world, as also the death of the Lord—three loudly crying mysteries that were completed in God's silence. 2How were they revealed to the aeons? A star shone in heaven, brighter than all the stars. Its light was inexpressible and its novelty caused amazement. All the other stars together with the sun and the moon gathered around the star in a roundel, and its light exceeded all of them. And confusion reigned about where the new and incomparable appearance was from. 3Following from this was the destruction of all magic and the disappearance of every bond of evil. Ignorance was eliminated; the old kingdom was eradicated when God appeared in human form for new, eternal life. What was prepared by God had its beginning. Henceforth was everything was put into commotion, because the destruction of death was taking place" (*Eph.* 19.1–3).

31. Pannenberg, *Grundzüge*, 264.

32. Camelot, *Ignace*, 88.

myth behind the words in *Eph.* 19 that Ignatius has reshaped into his own myth.[33] Without a doubt, one may not neglect the close connection in this verse with the history-of-religions notions of that time. There is here a similar symbolic presentation of the events of salvation as Paul presents them in the kenosis-thought of Phil 2:5-11. This myth should thus be understood as a naïve, vivid means of expression for an irrational event.[34] One must observe that this chapter is related to the struggle with false teaching and turns above all against the docetists who were already influenced by Gnosticism.[35] Ignatius fights for right belief with this expression that, from a dogmatic point of view, is rather dubious! The myth is only a means or a guise, with whose help indispensable Christian truth is expressed.

Ignatius does not speak often in his letters about the divine aspect in Christ. He probably considered a confession of this aspect so obvious that it did not need to be exposed or emphasized. The basics are found in the following verses:

- Jesus Christ . . . who was with the Father before all time and has appeared at the end (*Magn.* 6.1).

- One is physician, fleshly and spiritual, born and unborn, God appearing in the flesh, true life in death, both from Mary and from God, first passible and then impassible, Jesus Christ our Lord (*Eph.* 7.2).

- Wait expectantly for the one who is above time, the timeless one, the invisible one who became visible on account of us,

---

33. Schlier, *Religionsgeschichtliche Untersuchungen*, 5-81.

34. Lauha, *Otti orjan muodon*, 55.

35. Fischer, *Die apostolischen Väter*, 157n.85. Lietzmann sees the proclamation of the demise of paganism and the demonic powers in *Eph.* 19. "Die Sterne und ihre kosmische Macht, die Magie und der Dämonenglaube des Heidentums sind dem Ignatius reale Wirklichkeiten und keine blossen Bilder: aber ihre Überwindung durch die Gottesmacht in Christus ist ihm eine Realität, die er bewusst in ein analoges Bild kleidet, das nur darum gewählt ist, weil er den Sieg des Herrn über die bösen Geister lebendig zur Anschauung bringt" (Lietzmann, *Geschichte*, 261).

Faith

the intangible one, the impassible one who suffered on our account, Jesus Christ our Lord (*Pol.* 3.2).

- Son of God according to God's will and power (*Smyrn.* 1.1).

Christ possesses the same features as God. He has a pre-existence like the Father. He was with the Father before all time. His time is the timeless time of God who should not be bound with our familiar concept of time. God alone is unbegotten and unborn. Through him everything is created. Rackl has rightly indicated that the terms ἀγέννητος and ἄχρονος, taken together, are without a doubt a clear and unparalleled expression of absolute eternity and beginninglessness, although, of these two, only the last has sufficed for him to express completely eternity in the absolute sense.[36] Bousset takes hold of the latter two verses from the letters (*Eph.* 7.2; *Pol.* 3.2) and claims that they do not represent an "Asia Minor theology," or rather that they do not represent any particular theology, because these pieces of his view were drafted in accordance with the language of the Christ-hymn and community's belief.[37] If one assumes that Ignatius fights completely committedly for right belief and against false teaching, this comment appears incomprehensible. Does Ignatius not want to show in these verses what the unadulterated doctrine and the indissoluble truth are? One could think that, spurred by his enthusiasm, he so formulated his sentences that they sound like a hymn.

Ignatius's repeated comment on this question indicates the fierce fight that burned in the first centuries regarding the centrality of doctrine and regarding Christology. Christ is truly from David's seed but simultaneously from the Holy Ghost (*Eph.* 18.2) and from the line of David according to the flesh, Son of God according to God's will and power (*Smyrn.* 1.1). In these and similar expressions, the beginnings of the form of dogma are found whose most important later steps belong to the councils in Nicaea, Constantinople, Ephesus, and Chalcedon. In the Nicene-Constantinopolitan Creed, the essence of Christ is defined as true

---

36. Rackl, *Christologie*, 189.
37. Bousset, *Kyrios Christos*, 254–55.

Faith and Love in Ignatius of Antioch

God from true God, who took on flesh from the Holy Spirit and the Virgin Mary. However, it does not show further interest in the question of the relationship of the divine and human in Jesus. In the formula that the Council of Chalcedon created, it is emphasized that Christ is "one and the same" in two natures that must be considered without confusion, without change, without division, and without separation. The peculiarities of both natures cannot be blended into a unity nor can the contrast be abolished. Rather, they must be maintained separately but united in a person, the person of Jesus Christ. The significance of this creed lies crucially in the formula of two natures in one and the same person.[38] The first steps toward this doctrine of two natures, which later became dogma, are already to be found in Ignatian thought in the emphasis on the double origins of Jesus from God and from human beings.[39] At the same time, Ignatius has even been considered one of the men who further cultivated subordinationism.[40]

If the unity of God is very strongly emphasized in the creed from Chalcedon, it must be noted that this perspective is also represented in Ignatian thought (cf. 2.2 "The Unity of Faith"). In this respect, Ignatius has anticipated the development of theology or already apprehended at least the way that the church pursued in this area during the next centuries.

Ignatius's perception of God's silence, from which Christ should have proceeded, can provide a stimulus to comprehensive history-of-religions comparisons. Ignatius says, for example, "There is only one God who has revealed himself through his Son Jesus Christ, who is his Word that came forth from silence and was pleasing in every way to the one who sent him" (*Magn.* 8.2; cf. *Eph.* 15.1: There is, then, one teacher who, when he spoke, it happened, and what he did in silence is worthy of the Father). What

---

38. On the council in Chalcedon, cf. Seeberg, *Dogmenbildung*, 259–60.

39. Pannenberg, *Grundzüge*, 116. The views of Pannenberg and Loofs agree in this place.

40. Kettler, "Trinität," 1025. In the same context, Kettler notes that the relationship of the Spirit to the Father and Son still remain in abeyance in Ignatius, similarly as in Paul.

Faith

do these mysterious words mean? Must it be understood that God broke his silence after he was silent for a long time when he sent his Son into the world?[41] Or is the emergence from silence to be understood as a sudden transformation from non-manifestation to manifestation?[42] Or as a kind of protest against remaining too rigidly attached to literalism?[43] In any case, one can agree to the thought that σιγή, silence, should express the stillness that is the transcendent side in God.[44] Ignatius probably wanted to say that God is hidden, inaccessible, and entirely other than we picture him. He is surrounded by a holy silence in which we cannot penetrate, which suspends us with the words, "Take off your shoes!"

How should the countless history-of-religions parallels be assessed that can be found for the σιγή-thought?[45] Rüsch determined that the "procession of the Word from silence" is obviously gnostic-colored. However, that will not mean that the content of this way of thinking must be taken from Gnosticism.[46] Pannenberg's position is also similar. Behind Ignatius's formula, a perception must be recognized that can be inferred from gnostic doctrine, possibly from an evil Demiurge who has created the world. However, Pannenberg indicates similarly that the perception that is suggested by this formula does not correspond to Ignatius's concept.[47] Obvious-

---

41. Rackl, *Christologie*, 275.

42. Lightfoot, *Apostolic Fathers*, 2.2.127. "Christus ist Logos, sofern er dem vorgegangenen Schweigen Gottes Ende macht als 'unser einziger Lehrer', auf den schon die Propheten als seine Jünger gewartet haben" (Seeberg, *Anfänge*, 1.131).

43. Corwin, *St. Ignatius*, 124.

44. "He is the Source whence all life comes, the Reality to which all go at last. But he is transcendent in nature, and therefore unknown. However, to think of God as Silence is not for Ignatius to declare that he is finally inaccessible, for the Father 'revealed' himself in the Son, the Word came forth from Silence. Revelation is presented as the deliberate act of God, the ultimate act of divine condescension" (Corwin, *St. Ignatius*, 124).

45. The works by Corwin, Bartsch, and Schlier offer abundant material for comparison.

46. Rüsch, *Entstehung*, 50.

47. "Bei Ignatius von Antiochien heisst Jesus einmal in etwas anderem Sinne 'der Logos', nämlich als 'das Wort, in dem Gott sein Schweigen brach'

Faith and Love in Ignatius of Antioch

ly, Ignatius has employed the language and idiom of religions from that time but filled them with Christian content. It is also possible that biblical words are before his eyes in this verse in which there is talk about Jesus's silence.

A feature that Christian belief has in common with Gnosticism is the *mysterium tremendum*, the experience of God's holiness. This experience is representative for all religions. If Ignatius now emphasizes the significance of σιγή, he wants to underline God's holiness and protect the image of God from anthropomorphization and rationalization. With God's σιγή, Ignatius could refer to the time when there was not yet any revelation, when holy fear and expectation reigned among people, when no one yet knew anything about God's plans. In Christ this time of silence found its end. God spoke at that moment through his Son, and he revealed his salvific plan to people.

True God and true human—Ignatius's understanding of Christ is briefly summed up in this formulation. At the same time, a problem is introduced over which a more ardent fight burned in the next centuries. Ignatius did not develop Christology further. He only expressed what appeared to him to be most important. Thus, the possibility remained open for different interpretations. However, it was clear that one had to adhere both to the truly divine as well as to the truly human side of Christ. Christ is not a new God in a new cult community in the way that the gentile

---

(*Magn.* 8, 2). Hier ist im Hintergrund eine Gnostis zu vermuten, in der der Logos keine Schöpfer-, sondern nur Offenbarerfunktion hat, wohl eine dualistische Gnosis, die keinen Schöpfungsglauben kennt, für die vielmehr der Logos in eine fremde, vom bösen Demiurgen geschaffene Welt kommt. Das ist natürlich nicht die Vorstellung des Ignatius, aber sie ist deutlich hinter seiner Formulierung zu erkennen. Das Wort ist hier anders als bei Johannesprolog eher an das Schöpferswort denkt" (Pannenberg, *Grundzüge*, 161). One can hardly consider certain the thought that Ignatius's Logos-concept does not contain God as Creator. Has Ignatius rather accepted, differently from John, that the Logos was already in the first Creation? "Everything was made by him, and without him nothing was made that was made" (John 1:3).

Areopagita introduced this thought (σιγή) into Christian mysticism. θεῖα σιγὴ καὶ ἡσυχία reign in God. Whoever wants to be blessed with the divine explanation should renew his soul in stillness and quiet (Sormunen, *Pseudo-Dionysios Areopagita*, 43–44).

Faith

world understood him. He is the only way, the only truth, and he alone is the life. Only when we are found in Christ do we come to true life (*Eph.* 11.1). Christ is the first and the last, and eschatology and future hope are also tied to him alone.

2. The Unity of Faith

Ignatius writes to the community in Magnesia:

> So, as the Lord did nothing without the Father—being united with him—neither in his own person nor through the apostles, so also should you do nothing without the bishop and the presbyters. Do not try to let something appear reasonable to you (that you could do) privately. Rather, in a common assembly (profess) one prayer, one supplication, one mind, one hope in love, in which is blameless joy, that is, Jesus Christ, than whom nothing is better. All of you run together as to one temple of God, as to one altar, to one Jesus Christ, who came out from the Father and was with the one, and returned (to him) (*Magn.* 7.1–2).

The thought of unity is expressed very clearly in these words; it is one of the most important concerns for Ignatius and one of his central themes. The unity of God serves as a springboard. As Christ is one with the Father, so should believers also be one with one another. We also find this thought repeatedly in the Gospel of John (5:19, 30; 8:28; 12:49).

The root of this notion should obviously be sought in Jewish monotheism. Here, above all, is God's greatness, holiness, unapproachableness, and uniqueness emphasized. In Christian belief, Christ is coequal with God, and their unity is a basic truth of Christian faith from the beginning. However, Bartsch is of the opinion that the gnostic conception of God's unity stands in the middle of Ignatian thought. According to his view, Ignatius has opened the door in this way for the entrance of gnostic thought into the church.[48] However, that may not be entirely correct. In

---

48. "Der Gedanke der Einheit Gottes hat nicht in der biblischen Aussage

Ignatian thinking, biblical thought about the unity of God was the starting point. Even if one assumes that John the Evangelist was influenced by language that was cultivated in Gnosticism and perhaps also partly by gnostic ideas, it is rather improbable that John could have led someone like Ignatius to Gnosticism through his fundamentally gnostic thought. To confirm this, one could point to the Pauline heritage that Ignatius knew: One body and one Spirit . . . one Lord, one faith, one baptism; one God and Father of all, who is over all and through all and in all (Eph 4:4-6). The thought of God's unity is found repeatedly in the Bible. Therefore, it is in no way a purely gnostic notion.

The believers should thus love unity and shun division (*Phld.* 7.2; cf. *Magn.* 1.2; *Pol.* 1.2). Ignatius sees the negative influence of the false teachers precisely in that they destroy unity.[49] A division or fragmentation of the church means the loss of God's redemptive salvific acts. They are a shame for the church that cannot be put right. This forceful emphasis on the unity of Christians corresponds to the notion that found a fixed formulation in the Apostles' Creed. "I believe in one holy, universal church and in the communion of the saints . . ." On Ignatius's view, the church must fight against division with everything that it has. All powers are to be collected to build up and maintain unity.

The unity of Christians is chiefly a unity of faith and the struggle of faith for Ignatius. Rüsch formulated this thought aptly when he says that those who express themselves in faith and love become

---

von der Einzigkeit Gottes seine Wurzel, sondern in dem Einheitsprinzip der Gnosis, das dort Theologie und Soteriologie umfasst. Dieses umfassende Prinzip gnostischen Denkens war das Tor, durch das gnostische Gedankengänge und Mythologeme in die urchristliche Literatur eindrangen" (Bartsch, "Ignatius von Antiochien," 667). Bartsch treats this theme thoroughly in his work, *Gnostische Gut und Gemeindetradition*, 10–23. "Die Idee der Einheit Gottes hat ihren Grund in der griechischen Erkenntnis der Einheit der Welt, die aber für die Frömmigkeit erst durch die orientalischen Kulte fruchtbar wurde. Das hellenistische Judentum und die Gnosis spielen für Ignatius als Vermittler dieser Weltanschauung eine besondere Rolle" (Bartsch, *Gnostische Gut*, 52). Cf. Corwin, *St. Ignatius*, 136–37.

49. "Not only would the heretics deprive Ignatius of his Lord, but they disturbed the unity and harmony of the Church" (Richardson, *Christianity*, 8).

the personal unity.[50] For Christians of the early community, it was of immeasurable significance. They formed a small minority in gentile environs and must have needed to be able to rely on and support one another. Forms of spiritual life, like common prayer, worship service, and gatherings, urged the growth of the community and served reinforcement and edification in the present. To remain distant from the community was usually synonymous with a cessation in faith and love. Some left the community of saints from love of this world. Others ran back into a distinct world of thought and belief from which sectarianism could easily spring.

An isolation, even one that means well, has from the beginning always led to the division of the church. The solo action of a believer apart from the community could not be seen as blessed (εὔλογον). The danger of subjectivism is too great. To work together is necessary; otherwise, the believer remains without fruit. When one speaks so much today about "teamwork," it appears to conform well to Ignatius's notions. It is easier to find the way and the truth in a community than to search alone and groping. Together one also avoids more easily the danger of false ways. In the community, one is sheltered by various encounters with others from being encapsulated alone and from a narrowing of one's field of vision. According to Ignatius, sectarianism springs from isolation, going one's own way, and indulging in subjective ideas. Both unity in faith and unity in daily love are foundations of right Christian belief (cf. as well the designation "Life and Work," that is, the movement for practical Christianity that has often been considered characteristic of the ecumenical movement).

This unity also expresses itself as oneness. Ignatius admonishes this in many places and in a different context (for instance, *Magn.* 6.1; 15; *Phld.* 2.2: For many seemingly trustworthy wolves snatch away God's runners through wicked lust, but they will have no place in your unity). The following image is drawn from the realm of music and will illustrate the importance of unity. "But each of you should become a choir that you may be consonant in your harmony, take up God's melody in unity, and sing in one

---

50. Rüsch, *Entstehung*, 67.

voice to the Father through Jesus Christ so that he may hear you and recognize your good works as members of his Son. It is useful, therefore, if you live in flawless union so that you may also partake of God at all times" (*Eph.* 4.2; cf. *Rom.* 2.2). Some scholars have felt compelled by these and similar images and thoughts to ask whether Ignatius was a member of a mystery cult before he was a Christian. Choral singing was introduced to the church by Ignatius after he learned it, so it is reported, by watching the song of the angels in a vision. However in all likelihood, he had learned the musical traditions in the Jewish synagogue.[51] The image that Ignatius used is very clear. All choral singers are assigned to the conductor in tight discipline. The slightest deviation of a voice from the right melody causes the devaluation of the common musical performance. In a similar way, the community of Christians must stick together to be the community united in faith. Another image from music compares the conformity of believers with God's commands and will to the harmony of the strings of the zither (*Phld.* 1.2). The word in the original text, συνευρύθμισται, indicates that it appears to have the same rhythm.

Ignatius's language overflows with ever-new hortatory images and comparisons that should encourage the common fight. "Strive with one another, fight, run, suffer, sleep, raise one another up as God's stewards, attendants, and slaves" (*Pol.* 6.1). This image of struggle is idealized. As such, however, it emphatically expresses how great a value Ignatius laid on the unity of Christians. He does not grow weary of constantly urging unity. The same mindset that is characteristic of many later revival movements appears here. It is the common struggle and the common journeying in which everything is shared and borne in common in joy and song.

When Ignatius refers to all Christians participating in one Eucharist (*Phld.* 4), he emphasizes the unity that is to be experienced in Holy Communion. This is a matter of the deepest joining tie between Christians. Through union with Christ who suffered, died, and was raised, they are also unified with one another. This κοινωνία conquers all boundaries between people and unifies

---

51. Downey, *History*, 298.

Faith

Christians to the great community of pilgrims through all time.[52] We do not know the extent of Ignatius's conception here. "Be deliberate, therefore, to use one Eucharist—for the flesh of our Lord Jesus Christ is one and the cup of union with his blood is one, and the altar is one" (*Phld.* 4). Such an expressly proffered thought about the Eucharist suggests the assumption that Ignatius here understood the Eucharist as an intermediary between the redeemer and the co-wanderers.

Ignatius places harmonious unity in the community as a goal for believers to have in mind that must be achieved. He happily praises the Ephesians because they are so closely connected to their bishop, "like the church with Jesus Christ and like Jesus Christ with the Father, so that everything may be harmonious in unison" (*Eph.* 5.1). How this goal is to be achieved specifically, Ignatius does not here go on to consider. It is the community's task. However, as a church leader he must repeatedly point to the necessity of unity and oneness and always freshly set them before believers as the first task and the theme of daily struggle.

Whether the rationale or the theological motivation that Ignatius offers for the unity of God is sufficient and valid remains questionable. However, clear guidelines arise from Ignatius. What Christians know about the relationships of the persons of God in relation to one another must be emulated with reference to present human relations. God's unity must be a model for the unity of the community and the church. Neoplatonism later captured this way of thinking and developed it further. Here it becomes apparent that Ignatius delivered thoughts and notions based not only on Christian faith but also on philosophy. With regard to God's unity, no further conclusions can be drawn about Ignatius's views because the material that is available is inadequate. It can only be ascertained that Ignatius's notion converges with that of Gnosticism and also displays similarities with the image of God in mysticism.

---

52. "La communauté eucharistique est le sacrement de l'Unité; elle est le signe de l'amour unifiant à travers les siècles ceux qui s'ouvrent à son emprise" (Vial, *Ignace d'Antioche*, 84).

Faith and Love in Ignatius of Antioch

Johannes Quasten has pointed out that Ignatius uses the Pauline expression "to be in Christ." He wishes that believers "be found in Christ." It is characteristic for Ignatius that he always emphasizes that Christians are unified with Christ only if they are one with their bishop in faith and in obedience and particularly only when they participate in the worship service. He does not recognize personal independence in the spiritual life, for instance, in the way of a mystical union with Christ. Union with the Savior, according to Ignatius, is only possible in connection with the worship service, liturgy, and Eucharist.[53] Quasten rightly emphasizes the mundane ecclesial line of Ignatius's Christ-mysticism. For Ignatius, there are no wonderful mystical experiences of an individual Christian because the Christian is deceived by them through illusions and subjectivity. There is for him only the common struggle of faith in the Lord's community. A true unity of Christians is only possible inside of the church.

This sort of unity is defined by faith and love; they provide unity with its character that regulates it and points it on its way.[54] Ignatius expressly refers to the union of faith with love when he speaks about the union of Jesus Christ's flesh and spirit (*Magn.* 1.1). This union with Christ is, however, always only possible through participation in the sacred worship service of their communion and, through this, that everything which occurs in the Christian's life agrees with the tenets of faith and love.

A characteristic appearance in contemporary Christianity that represents similar tenets is the ecumenical movement. It is gaining currency in ever-wider circles. Even the Roman Catholic Church is showing interest in this question. For instance, Joseph Lortz, its most significant church historian today, laments the division of Christianity in his work *Geschichte der Kirche*. He appears to approve wholeheartedly of the ecumenical movement. Ignatius's

---

53. Quasten, *Patrology*. 1.72–73.

54. "Ἐνωσις has to do at once with the union of the believer and God in faith and love, and with the unity of Christians in faith and worship. . . . Unity in the church is secured by a union of faith and love, or of belief in regard to the life, death and resurrection of Christ" (Torrance, *Doctrine of Grace*, 71).

Faith

thoughts and views illustrate that these questions and problems are not new, that already in the earliest times of the church the significance of the unity of all Christians was recognized and ways to its attainment were sought.

3. Faith and Church Office

The most important part of Ignatius's lifework is the expansion and consolidation of the ecclesial office, particularly with regard to the monarchial episcopate. The difficulties with which the young church had to fight have already been alluded to. The greatest was the impending danger from the side of false doctrine. It stepped insidiously and surreptitiously from the inside of the church and confused minds all the more. The power of the state, which was antagonistically disposed to Christians, threatened it from the outside. What should one do in this situation?

> Let there be nothing in you that is capable of dividing you but rather be unified with the bishop and those who preside in the image and teaching of immortality (*Magn.* 6.2).

The bishops, who were at the top of the church, stand at the foremost front in this struggle. Their existence, their office, and their authority were an irreplaceable help in these disputes. The episcopacy meant protection both against false doctrine and also against public persecutions.[55]

However, such a commonly formed front under the bishop's guidance against the dangers threating from outside now demanded that the church obey this leader and that he must be honored. "We clearly must view the bishop as the Lord himself" (*Eph.* 6.1). This sentence brings to expression the thought that the bishops in the church are the Lord's representatives who lead their office with

---

55. "External factors may also have influenced the development of the episcopate by making it plain that a strong and ordered ministry of this sort was necessary for the protection of Christians both from heresy (notably Gnosticism) and from official persecution" (Downey, *History*, 297).

the full power given by the highest Shepherd.[56] The true head of the church, however, is God himself and Jesus Christ. "Therefore, we should take pains not to oppose the bishop so that we may be subject to God" (*Eph.* 5.3). Ignatius thus urges the same deference and the same obedience to the bishop as to God. A "soft line" does not help when it fights for the greatest values. Just as discipline is necessary in an army if military operations are to have success, so it must also be for Christians who fight against the evil and hostile world if they should succeed in victory—that is the view of Ignatius.

The admonitions to subjection and obedience to the bishop recur ceaselessly with the most varied rationales. "It is good to acknowledge God and the bishop. Whoever honors the bishop has been honored by God. Whoever does something behind the bishop's back serves the devil" (*Smyrn.* 9.1). The recognition of the bishop's authority is also presented as aesthetically desirable and as a beautiful (καλῶς) thing. However, acting behind the bishop's back is deeply reprehensible and a service to the devil. The bishop is also entitled to know everything that happens in the community. "Therefore, it is necessary that nothing be undertaken without the bishop" (*Trall.* 2.2; *Phld.* 7.2; *Magn.* 7.1). "Be submissive to the bishop and to one another, as Jesus Christ was to the Father according to the flesh, and the apostles to Christ, the Father, and the Spirit" (*Magn.* 13.2). It is regarded as imperative to show obedience with undivided mind to the bishop and the presbytery and to break bread in common (*Eph.* 20.2). It is demanded from every Christian to be obedient and closely connected with the bishop and the presbytery in unanimous subordination (*Eph.* 2.2).

Ignatius gives the rational for such an elevated place for the bishop in the following way. The bishop presides in God's place (*Magn.* 6.1), and the bishop is the type of the Father (*Trall.* 3.1). Obedience to God is thus connected to obedience to the highest representative of the church, the bishop—a thought that the Catholic Church has incorporated and developed further. The

---

56. The shepherd motif: But where the shepherd is, follow there as sheep (*Phld.* 2.1).

Faith

authority of the office therefore has a solid tradition. The question now arises, did Ignatius think that the outer order demanded obedience to the bishop or is there also a reason for obedience and honor in the holiness of the office? Obviously for Ignatius the office itself has its own considerable value. The bishop is not the only leading man in the struggle for the rights of the community. Rather, he is simultaneously the representative of God and Jesus Christ on earth and a representative who deserves the corresponding honor and deference. This place lifts him out of the crowd of people and the community members. Thus, as Paul says that he has not obtained his assignment from men or through men but through Jesus Christ and God the Father (Gal 1:1), so also Ignatius invokes this authority from above. He determined that a bishop did not attain the service to the community through people or due to a vain thirst for glory but in the love of God the Father and the Lord Jesus Christ (*Phld.* 1.1). Whether fundamental differences persist between the places of Paul and Ignatius on this question or whether they differ only in detail cannot be solved with the available material. However, Ignatius always emphasizes the significance of the office, so often that it is really a characteristic feature for him.

The rights and authorities of the bishop are quite comprehensive according to Ignatius. It is not permitted to baptize or to celebrate the love feast without the bishop. What the bishop approves is also pleasing to God so that what believers do may be secure and valid (*Smyrn.* 8.2). The bishop should also confer approval for marriage so that the marriage conforms to the Lord and not to lust (*Pol.* 5.2). To his fellow minister Polycarp, he gives the advice, "Nothing should happen without your consent. Also, do nothing without God, even as you are already doing" (*Pol.* 4.1). The bishop is thus the one who oversees all important ecclesial ceremonies.[57]

---

57. "Die Leitung der Einzelgemeinde soll ganz und gar in der Hand dieses einen Bischofs liegen, der alle ihre Lebensbetätigungen in Gang setzt und beaufsichtigt, ohne den keine kirchliche Handlung Gültigkeit hat und der kraft seines Amtes, und sei er auch jung an Jahren und unvollkommen in seinem Wesen, jeder Beanstandung entzogen ist" (Bauer, *Rechtgläubigkeit und Ketzerei*, 66).

Even without anything further, it is insightful that oversight is necessary for the proper execution and preservation of the dignity of sacred services, especially when the ecclesial standards at that time were not yet defined and ordered in all things and here or there it could easily come to disorder or arbitrariness. It seems strange to us today that the granting of permission for marriage was reserved for the bishop alone. Still, reasons can be found for this. First, Jewish-Old Testament patriarchal tradition appears to have still been quite active in the first communities of the first Christians. The most important steps in life had to be permitted by the father in the family and by their leader in the community. One trusted the decisions of the presbyters. Referring to them was simply essential. A further problem was the question of mixed marriages. How should one view a marriage between a Christian and a pagan? It was preferable that both spouses were Christians, but this could not be made compulsory for all. It was also necessary to consider whether the preconditions for a Christian family life and for a Christian raising of children were fulfilled. The bishop should specifically decide this question for each case. The right of the bishop to decide about permission for marriage and mixed marriages probably also had a further ground in the fourth commandment, as surely in Christian communities, particularly in those with Jewish tradition, the commandments were generally viewed as mandatory. At root, therefore, it does not concern a human right but a divine one.

It was assumed at that time that a bishop supervised all ecclesial activities in the community. Yet on this point, one must bear in mind that the jurisdiction of a bishop in the time of Ignatius was not large. He therefore had a chance to assign someone else to supervise the eucharistic celebration if he did not have time to be there (*Smyrn.* 8.1). The bishop was a man who held a responsible and leading place in the community.[58] The bishop of a community at that time was thus rather like the first pastor in a community

---

58. "Varje församlings herde kallas alltså biskop" (Andrén, *Apostoliska fäderna*, 96–97).

Faith

today or possibly also like the dean.[59] The number of community members varied. However, if one measures the size of the communities by today's scales, they were quite small.

The ideal personal characteristics of a bishop are described in the letter to the Trallians. "For I have received the example of your love, and I have it with you in the person of your bishop, whose attitude is a great lesson and whose gentleness is power, whom even the godless, I believe, respect" (*Trall.* 3.2). Although one generally receives an image that depicts the bishop keeping the foundations of right belief resolutely, securely, and himself, there is, besides this, also an image of the leader of the church visibly characterized by love and gentleness. Faith and love always go hand in hand. Is the characteristic of love in the ideal bishop perhaps a Johannine legacy? Ignatius knew the influence of John's personality, his spirit, his thought, and his notions. All that left deep impressions on him and obviously contributed to his image of the bishop. He should reflect the Savior's love and benevolence. He should generate esteem in his environment, even if it is pagan. In a similar way, Paul required the Christian walk to be an outward witness for people (Col 4:5; 1 Thess 4:12; 1 Tim 3:7).

The verses in which the silence of the bishops is discussed are difficult to interpret. "The more one sees that the bishop is silent, the more one should stand in awe of him" (*Eph.* 6.1), Ignatius writes. Further, "I am wholly amazed at his tenderness, who can do more by being silent than those who speak idle words" (*Phld.* 1.1). Ignatius points out that Jesus was also silent; should the bishops possibly be disciples of their Master here? "The one who truly possesses Jesus's word can also hear his silence so that he may be complete, so that he may act through his word and be known through his silence" (*Eph.* 15.2; cf. "... through his Son Jesus Christ, who is his Word proceeding from silence and who pleased the one who sent him in everything;" *Magn.* 8.2). The discussion of God's silence, σιγή, has already taken place. It regards that which indicates transcendence and mysticism. Ignatius may be of the view that, if

---

59. "Ihr Bereich scheint auch die zu den Städten gehörenden Landbezirke zu umfassen" (Adam, "Kirchenverfassung," 1535).

Faith and Love in Ignatius of Antioch

one speaks of God's σιγή, one must bestow this σιγή also on Jesus Christ because the Father and Son are one.[60] From there it is then only a small step to the bishops, who are representatives of God and Christ, and an entire hierarchy of silence emerges. A line leads from God through Christ to the bishops. It is debatable whether the origin for this notion is Hellenistic mysticism, biblical thought (God rested [Gen 2:2]; Jesus's silence), or a combination of both.[61] However, there are very practical explanations for the silence of the bishops. Had a bishop perhaps given ground or lacked something like the gift of oratory or generally the necessary abilities for the exercise of the office that had forced to him to a life in stillness?[62] There is no clear answer to this question. It is probably that the concept of σιγή in Ignatius has been influenced by Hellenistic mysticism but that the biblical notion is more strongly prevalent. Fischer refers to Ignatius's remarks in *Eph.* 6.1 and *Phld.* 1.1 and discerns that the silent bishop is probably an image and imitator of the silent God and silent pre-existent Christ.[63] On this view, "the

60. "Zwischen dem Vater und dem Sohn herrscht eine lebendige Analogie im Schweigen" (Bieder, " Deutung," 36).

61. "Es ist ohne weiteres ersichtlich, dass Ignatius in bedenklicher Nähe bei dieser hellenistischen Unio mystica des Schweigens sich aufhält. Ist das kirchliche Schweigen nur ein Abbild des göttlichen Schweigens, ist die Kirche der Mikrokosmos der göttlichen Welt, ist sie in ihrer schweigenden Anbetung gen Himmel offen (H. Chadwick, "The Silence of Bishops in Ignatius." *Harvard Theological Review* 43 [1950] 170), dann ist zu fragen, ob diese gottesdienstlich gefüllte hellenistische Mystik der schweigenden Anbetung noch etwas von der Ruhe des biblischen Gottes erahnen lässt, oder ob sie nur im Gegensatz zu dieser biblisch göttlichen Ruhe verstanden werden kann" (Bieder, "Deutung," 38).

62. "Why was the bishop of Ephesus 'silent'? Lightfoot speaks of 'the quiet and retiring disposition of the bishop,' while Bauer suggests that he did not have 'the gift of eloquence.' H. Chadwick, on the other hand, considers all the passages in which Ignatius speaks of silence and concludes that here he is alluding to the bishop's likeness to God, of whom one characteristic is silence. . . . P. Meinhold argues that the Ephesians, like the Philadelphians (1:1) are concerned about a bishop who lacks spiritual gifts, cannot pray or prophesy spiritually, and is forced to remain silent. In Meinhold's view Ignatius defend the bishop by interpreting his silence in semi-Gnostic fashion" (Grant, *Ignatius*, 37).

63. Fischer, *Die apostolischen Väter*, 147. Meinhold also represents this view ("Schweigende Bischöfe," 489).

Faith

silent bishops" are disciples of the highest biblical models. This is a quite reasonable position, although no absolutely certain evidence can be adduced for its correctness.

One considers Ignatius the first significant representative of the monarchial episcopate. Phenomena that point in this direction already emerged before Ignatius. Thus, someone like Jürgen Roloff raises the question whether the office of the apostles' disciples do not, as represented in the Pastoral Epistles, already lead in the way of the monarchial episcopacy.[64] *1 Clement*, which dates back to 96 or 97 CE, emphasizes the significance of the bishop's office (*1 Clem.* 42, 44). God sent Christ, the apostles received the gospel from him, and they appointed bishops. Ignatius's letters already assume single bishops at the top of the community and view the monarchial episcopacy as an institution that is taken for granted.[65] That also arises from the verses cited above that deal with the place of a bishop and his rights.

This development led to an exclusive control for the bishop over an ecclesial sphere. All the power of the council of presbyters gradually fell to the bishop. It is striking that the office is nowhere based on apostolic succession.[66] The monarchial episcopacy occupied a secure place in the Asian community at this time. In absolutely none of these communities is a majority of men found at the head; one, the bishop, is leader everywhere.[67]

Catholic scholars are agreed about Ignatius's significance as the creator and consolidator of the monarchial episcopacy. The majority of Protestant scholars also regard the emergence of the monarchial episcopate as Ignatius's chief credit. Only Walter Bauer represents a divergent opinion. He alleges that Ignatius depicts a desirable portrait of the ideal that in no way corresponds to the

---

64. Roloff, *Apostolat—Verkündigung—Kirche*, 251.

65. Altaner, *Patrologie*, 86; Funk and Bihlmeyer, *Kirchengeschichte*, 74. "Schliesslich haben wir in den Ignatianen einen Nachweis darüber, dass bereits im ersten Jahrzehnt des 2. Jahrhunderts in einigen Gemeinden der Asia der monarchische Episkopat mindestens ansatzsweise vorhanden war . . ." (Roloff, *Apostolat—Verkündigung—Kirche*, 251).

66. Adam, "Bischof," 1301–2.

67. Knopf, *Das nachapostolische Zeitalter*, 210.

prevailing circumstances.[68] The general approach is that the phenomena that point to a monarchial episcopacy were already present before Ignatius but that Ignatius first elaborated these thoughts precisely in detail and specified a clear doctrine. The beginnings of the monarchial episcopacy are already suggested in what appears as far back as the Pastoral Epistles. Revelation 2 and 3 should also be mentioned in this context. The guardian angel of the community here appears as the bishop's heavenly partner.[69] The tenuous source material complicates matters for the scholar to make a complete picture of the origin and development of the episcopacy. There were obviously events in this development about which we possess no news. However, it must be assumed that Ignatius could not write his doctrine of the episcopacy with such an unconcerned certainty if this episcopacy did not correspond to real facts in the community.

This place of the bishop was obviously not yet clear and recognized by all at the time of Ignatius. Otherwise, Ignatius would hardly have laid such emphatic value on establishing a consistent doctrine in this matter. He operates in a pioneering fashion and must strive and struggle to establish his new ideas, ideas toward which many were still full of mistrust.

A fashion of interpreters is the question of the bishop's place and the community in Rome. In the prescript of his *Romans*, Ignatius speaks of the church that conforms to the faith and love of Jesus Christ and that also presides in the place of the territory of the Romans (προκάθηται ἐν τόπῳ χωρίου Ῥωμαίων). Walter Bauer refers to Eusebius and suggests that Christians in the city of Rome would have had the practice from the beginning of helping all other Christians in diverse ways with good deeds and also of always offering support to countless other communities in whatever cities. The old custom was continued by the bishop at that time.[70] Quasten refers to this view and recalls that it was already repre-

---

68. Bauer, *Rechtgläubigkeit und Ketzerei*, 65; Lohse, "Ignatius von Antiochien," 287.

69. Adam, "Bischof," 1301.

70. Bauer, *Rechtgläubigkeit und Ketzerei*, 125.

Faith

sented by Harnack, but he clarifies that it does not satisfy him. He primarily invokes Johannes Thiele's thought on this problem and supposes that the word "love" in this context must be construed much more broadly than it commonly is. The precedence in love (προκαθημένη τῆς ἀγάπης) should thus be understood as indicating the leading position of the Roman church in Christianity.[71] Many scholars are not certain how Ignatius's thought should be clarified in this verse and leave the question open.[72] One can consider Fischer's statement as a reasonable compromise. According to him, it is not sufficient, when one represents the view on the Protestant side, for this verse to be a discourse only about a moral primacy that the community in Rome has achieved through a caritative disposition and acts of love for the neighbor. The expression is mostly likely rightly understood if one interprets it as that the Roman church is "the leading, decisive authority in which the essence of Christianity is recognized" (J. Thiele). However, Fischer points out that Ignatius does not speak in relation to the bishop of the Roman clergy.[73] Although both Quasten and Fischer invoke the same scholars, they still do not come to the same conclusion in the end. Fischer points out that the talk in this verse is not about an

---

71. "Then Ignatius would by the phrase 'presiding in love' assign to the Roman church authority to guide and lead in that which constitutes the essence of Christianity and of the new order brought into the world by Christ's divine love for men. . . . Roman Church is acknowledged by Ignatius as her due, and is founded not on the extent of her charitable influence but on her inherent right to universal ecclesiastical supremacy" (Quasten, *Patrology*, 1.70). Altaner, another Catholic scholar and author of a general work of Patrology, represents a similar opinion. "Das besondere Ansehen und eine tatsächliche Vorrangstellung der römischen Gemeinde ist bereits deutlich zu spüren" (Altaner, *Patrologie*, 130).

72. "Det är ovisst i vilket avseende Ignatius menar, att Roms kyrka intar den främsta platsen" (Andrén, *Apostoliska fäderna*, 85). "This is not the place to rehearse the argument for and against such an acceptation, and it is enough to say that true meaning of the celebrated phrase is still an open question" (Richardson, *Christianity*, 134).

73. Fischer, *Die apostolischen Väter*, 130. "Die Übersetzung ist im höchsten Grade fragwürdig, und die Erklärung ist durchaus unzulässig, weil sie den Begriff des Vorsitzens verflüchtigt, das προκαθημένη seiner eigentlichen Bedeutung beraubt" (Bardenhewer, *Geschichte der altkirchlichen Literatur*, 1.120).

Faith and Love in Ignatius of Antioch

actual primacy of doctrine or jurisdiction.[74] However, Quasten is right that the primacy of Rome must be grounded differently than only through this primacy of love. According to Ignatius, faith also belongs to this. In summary, one can say that Ignatius appreciates the community in Rome and its Christians and allocates them a place of honor in the world at that time on account of their faith and their love. The Ignatian letters do not allow further conclusions than this.

The community belongs in close connection with the bishop's office. The concept of the catholic church (καθολικὴ ἐκκλησία) emerges for the first time in this context. This concept does not yet appear with the legal and confessional fixedness with which it is used in later times.[75] "Wherever the bishop appears, there should the congregation be, just as, wherever Christ Jesus is, there the entire community (catholic church) is" (*Smyrn.* 8.2). The designation "catholic church" does not mean here a general church in opposition to the false teachers and sects.[76] It is concerned much more to emphasize the difference that exists between the general church and the local church that is composed under the bishop.[77] Like Christ the Lord, it also encompasses the entire globe.[78] Ignatius has not developed his doctrine of the church further. Still, the beginnings of the creed are already seen clearly: I believe in one holy catholic church, in the communion of the saints, . . . in one holy and apostolic church. The doctrine of a general catholic church is only in the making, but Ignatius already recognizes how communities, which will be a great communion of the saints that

---

74. Fischer, *Die apostolischen Väter*, 130.

75. Rüsch, *Entstehung*, 55.

76. Lightfoot, *Apostolic Fathers*, 2.2.310.

77. "Im Gegensatz zu der unter dem bischof verfassten Ortsgemeinde spricht Ignatius—und seine Briefe sind das älteste Dokument dieses Sprachgebrauches—von der allgemeinein Kirche welche auch schlechtweg die Kirche heisst" (Zahn, *Ignatius von Antiochien*, 428). "Der Herr der 'katholischen Kirche' ist Jesus Christus, und 'katholisch' bezeichnet hier nur die gesamte Menge der Gläubigen im Gegensatz nur Einzelgemeinde" (Knopf, *Das nachapostolische Zeitalter*, 220).

78. Seeberg, *Anfänge*, 1.231.

Faith

will know neither geographic nor other borders, are universally portrayed under one Lord.

Earlier it was noted that Ignatius represents monarchial episcopacy. The bishop alone has the right to all important decisions in the affairs of the community.[79] However, Ignatius also knows of other ecclesial offices in addition to the bishop. "All of you follow the bishop as Jesus Christ followed the Father, and the presbytery as the apostles. But regard the deacons as God's command!" (*Smyrn.* 8.1). The bishop, the presbytery, and the deacons are often mentioned. One should pay attention to them (*Phld.* 7.1), be one with them (*Phld.* inscr.), accept a subordinate role to them (*Pol.* 6.1), and do nothing without them (*Trall.* 7.1–2; cf. *Magn.* 6.1; 13.1; *Smyrn.* 12.2). The presbytery is connected to the bishop like the strings of the harp (*Eph.* 4.1), and it appears to be after the bishop in the next position with regard to prestige. Ignatius sometimes emphasizes obedience to the presbytery in a quite particular way (*Trall.* 2.2; 3.1; *Magn.* 7.1).

Precisely in which way the presbyters function cannot be clearly seen from Ignatius's letters. Perhaps the presbyters form the group that exercises the bishop's proxy.[80] The deacons and their work should also be respected, but they have to accept a subordinate position to the bishop and presbyters. Yet the concept of the diaconate appears to have changed to a really great extent since New Testament times. In this respect, Christ's model—for he did not come to be served but to serve and to give his life as a ransom for many (Matt 20:28)—has almost entirely faded. That shows clearly that, in Ignatius, the martyr-ideal has replaced the ideal of the diaconate for serving Christianity.

---

79. "An der Spitze jeder Gemeinde (mit Ausnahme der römischen, an die er schreibt) steht ein Bischof, der diesen und keinen anderen Namen führt. Er ist der wirkliche Monarch der Gemeinde, wie es schweint, in jeder denkbaren Beziehung" (Harnack, *Entstehung und Entwicklung*, 19). Nils Johansson points to this view of Harnack ("Till frågan om ämbetets kontinuitet i fornkyrkan," 169). However, he determines that Harnack also emphasizes this "democratic" feature. The office holders had been sent and recognized by a particular community.

80. Meinhold, "Schweigende Bischöfe," 488–9.

Faith and Love in Ignatius of Antioch

Ignatius's notion constitutes a new phase in the understanding of ecclesial office. The bishop, the elder, and the deacon have stepped into the place of the apostle, the prophet, and the teacher. The development toward institutionalization can be clearly followed here. Nils Johansson is, however, right to note that these later offices should not be understood less spiritually than earlier offices. Both the apostles and the bishops were appointed by God on the view of the first Christians, and both needed a charisma to be able to rightly accomplish their assignments.[81]

Ignatius saw the development of offices as linear. It occurred without disruptive factors in his view.

> Therefore, be eager to stand firm in the commands of the Lord and the apostles so that you may prosper in everything that you do in flesh and spirit, in faith and love, in the Son and Father and in the Spirit, in the beginning and the end, with your most worthy bishop and your presbytery, which is a worthily-woven spiritual crown, and your godly deacons (*Magn.* 13.1).

The ordinances (δόγματα) of the Lord and the apostles stand in the first place, and the office of the bishop, presbyters, and deacons come after that. A close connection exists between these two sides.[82] The offices of the church therefore belong with the foundation of the church. They represent the highest authority in the community.

Fischer points out that the place of the clergy is grounded in a speculative-mystical manner. The three-tiered earthly hierarchy should be a type of the heavenly hierarchy of God the Father, Christ, and the apostles. However, they are not only the type but, more than that, a visible representation of the heavenly hierarchy because the church is already a heavenly-earthly community.[83]

---

81. Johansson, "Till frågan om ämbetets kontinuitet i fornkyrkan," 172.

82. "Betont wird, besonders bei Ignatius (Ign. *Magn.* 13, vgl. Ign. *Trall.* 7, 1), der wesenhafte Zusammenhang zwischen den 'dogmata' des Kyrios und der Apostel und dem Amt des Bischofs, der Presbyter und Diakone" (Rahner and Lehmann, "Kerygma und Dogma," 1.641).

83. Fischer, *Die apostolischen Väter*, 127.

Faith

This line leads to the sacramental-hierarchical understanding of ecclesial office.[84] To what degree did Ignatius follow it? Did he want to highlight this character of the church office or did he consider practical considerations more important in this context, perhaps that the ecclesial offices are necessary as a defensive front against false teachers?[85] Obviously Ignatius is affected by both points of view. The persecuted church should fight effectively against the threat of false teachers and be able to defend their rights. Therefore, a leader is needed with sufficient authority, a "monarchial head," a bishop, who then must have the necessary number of "subordinate leaders," namely, the presbyters and deacons at his disposal.

However, the ecclesial office is not only there for the sake of order. It is appointed by God; the office holders act with divine authority that the community has mediated and entrusted to them. Ignatius has not developed the sacramental-hierarchical definition of office, but he has clearly brought to expression that the ecclesial office is a direct extension of the work that the Lord himself began on earth. Therefore, the same respect and the same obedience are to be brought to the office holders, particularly the bishop, as to the Lord, the founder of the church.

Ignatius's thoughts about the church and its office always re-emerge through the centuries. In the second century, for example, Irenaeus refers to quite similar things as hallmarks of the church. Thus he indicates in his famous book *Adversus haereses* that the Lord must judge all who provoke schisms. They cut up the great and glorious body of Christ into pieces for petty, invalid reasons and would like to kill it inasmuch as it lies with them. One

---

84. Bardenhewer represents the view that Ignatius's letters are witnesses for the Catholic Church order, the primacy of the church in Rome, the monarchical organization of Christian communities, and the three sacramental levels of the hierarchy (*Geschichte der altkirchlichen Literatur*, 1.122).

85. "Die Zentralisierung des Versammlungswesens und seine Unterstellung unter den Bischof und die andern Amtsträger ist ihm die Panacee gegen alle Härese" (Knopf, *Das nachapostolische Zeitalter*, 214). This is a point of view about which all scholars are agreed. Order and discipline also belong to the essence of the church. If they fail, one gets into chaos and anarchy. "For God is not a God of disorder but of peace" (1 Cor 14:33).

Faith and Love in Ignatius of Antioch

recognizes the body of Christ by following the bishop, whom the apostles delivered to the entire church.[86] Pseudo-Dionysius Areopagita writes in his *Ecclesial Hierarchy* that, as the entire hierarchy culminates in Jesus as its goal and endpoint, so also each individual hierarchy culminates in its bishop who has been filled by God.[87]

As mentioned above, Ignatius concedes a special place to Rome because it possess a precedence in love. Eusebius recounts in his church history that Dionysius, the bishop of Corinth, praised the church in Rome for the love that they showed to all the brothers in a variety of ways.[88] This rationale of Ignatius is thus likewise found in later times. However, it is not mentioned in the church fathers to support Roman primacy. Scholars presented that in this way initially. Leo the Great grounded Rome's authority with Jesus's words to Peter, who should have been the first bishop of Rome. ("You are Peter and on this rock I will build my community"; Matt 16:18). John Chrysostom points to the stay of Peter and Paul in Rome. If there are varieties of opinion about the right reading of Ignatius's words in this context, it is still certain that these words were an impetus for the higher estimation of Rome and for the rise of the Roman bishop to Pope, the leader of Christendom.

Meinhold has determined that Ignatius had opponents in different communities whose hostile disposition to monarchial episcopacy and the two other ecclesial offices was mutual. It happened that the prophets and teachers caused degeneration, appearing as wandering preachers who wreaked abuse with their spiritual quality.[89] All this was reason enough to emphasize the significance of the ecclesial offices in the community. Only in the

---

86. Heilmann and Kraft, *Texte der Kirchenväter*, 4.33–34. Sormunen writes about Irenaeus, "Er war der erste Kirchenführer, der schon deutlich in den Ignatianischen Briefen den Gedanken über die Notwendigkeit des 'Katholizismus' der Kirche für das Fortbestehen des christlichen Glaubens sah" (*Dogmihistoria*, 71).

87. Heilmann and Kraft, *Texte der Kirchenväter*, 4.149.

88. Ibid., 4.113–14.

89. Meinhold, "Schweigende Bischöfe," 485–86; Roloff, *Apostolat—Verkündigung—Kirche*, 208.

Faith

office did Ignatius find the secure footing with whose help the church could remain steadfast and upright even in dangers and difficulties. However, a more important reason exists to rely on the ecclesial office. The biblical canon was still in the making; the Holy Scriptures were lacking that could signify they had an absolute authority. In this situation, there appeared to be no other possibility than that which the bishop of Antioch chose.[90] With it, he wanted the best for the church, he thought about the future, and he caught sight of God's leadership and conduct in the development of the ecclesial office.

4. Faith and Prayer

Only a little is found regarding the spiritual life in Ignatius's letters, and what he has to say is not particularly multifaceted. At this point, however, one must bear in mind that Ignatius is going to meet death. In such a situation, one mentions only the most important matters and tacitly assumes what is self-evident. Prayer—conversation with God—belongs to these things that are important and worth mentioning for Ignatius. For Ignatius, there is no spiritual life without prayer. Rackl is of the opinion that Ignatius is a mystic in this respect.[91] If one understands "mystic" in

---

90. Ignatius has his *corpus Paulinum*, the collection of the Pauline letters. In his time, Polycarp has his *corpus Ignatianum*, the letters of Ignatius (Haag, "Die Buchwerdung des Wortes Gottes," 1.381). The latest news that stems from Polycarp himself (Pol. *Phil.* 13) is cogent, but it is extremely uncertain to what extent Ignatius has copies of the Pauline letters. However, he knows the Pauline thought well.

91. "Ignatius ist in der Tat Mystiker. Wenn es wahr ist, dass das mystische Leben nichts anderes ist als 'das Leben in Gott', und wenn das christlich-mystische Leben nichts anderes bedeutet als dies, 'dass wer in Gott leben will, danach trachten wird, mit Christus, in Christus zu leben—mit Christus, weil er uns Wahrheit und Weg, in Christus, weil er uns Leben ist, wahres, reiches, göttliches Leben'; wenn das die Meinung der hohen Meister der Mystik gewesen ist, dann war Ignatius ein Mystiker und zwar ein christlicher Mystiker im vollem Sinne des Wortes" (Rackl, *Christologie*, 204). Fischer considers Ignatius a mystic. "Es geht Ignatius immer und überall um möglichst innige Vereinigung mit Christus und dem Vater" (Fischer, *Die apostolischen Väter*, 136). This

the broadest sense of the word, as striving to lead a hidden life with God and Jesus Christ, as interiority and intimacy, then Ignatius is in fact a mystic specifically in the area of prayer.

Ignatius rebukes those who remain distant from the eucharistic celebration and prayer (*Smyrn.* 7.1). For him, the community is a *communio* that is held together by fellowship around the Lord's table and through common prayer—a notion that is typical for the first Christian communities. The Eucharist and prayer form the core of spiritual life. Whoever no longer participates in it, their faith dies and their inner life atrophies.

Ignatius urges Polycarp to dedicate himself to ceaseless prayers (ἀδιαλείπτοις; *Pol.* 1.3; cf. *Eph.* 10.1). A clear echo of Pauline thought is found here (1 Thess 5:17; 1 Cor 7:5). Ignatius knows that the time that remains for him is short, and he is living the rest of his life hour by hour conscious that a Christian cannot go one step forward without help from above and without protection. Ignatius urges his friends to hold steady in prayer from the experience that such help and strength are obtained from above through prayer.

Ignatius appeals again and again to the community members and asks for their prayer. He appears to trust in the strength of this prayer. "Your prayer has gone out to the church at Antioch in Syria . . . because they have already reached a harbor by your prayer" (*Smyrn.* 11.1, 3). The image of the harbor here signifies quiet, as opposed to stormy, seas.[92] The persecutions have stopped, and the prayers of the beleaguered community have been heard. The discourse in *Phld.* 10.1 and *Pol.* 7.1 likewise regards the same thing. The view has been advocated that this verse does not concern relief from external persecution but rather the elimination of inner-communal difficulties.[93] However, this explanation is too "spiritual." The time of Trajan (98–117) was notoriously a difficult time for Christians, although no universal, great persecutions occurred

---

link expresses itself directly in the life of prayer.

92. Fischer, *Die apostolischen Väter*, 215.

93. This opinion is represented by Harrison, *Polycarp's Two Epistles*, 79, 106; Fischer, *Die apostolischen Väter*, 203.

Faith

in this time. Trajan explains to Pliny the Younger, who appealed to Caesar with a question regarding Christians, that to be a Christian is a crime worthy of death. Although Christians were not allowed to be tracked and anonymous declarations could not be heeded, everyone that refused state sacrifices fell under judgment.[94] Local persecutions were obviously nothing unusual, and it appears to have been such a locally confined persecution here. Ignatius had every reason to view the dawn of an easier time as the answer to heartfelt prayers. By mentioning these events, Ignatius also wants to let others participate in the joy. In addition, the "prayer front" is strengthened in which Christians of the second century were allied for one another and for the kingdom of God.

"Remember me in your prayers, so that I may obtain God, and also the church in Syria—whose name I am not worthy to bear. I still need your unified prayer in God and your love" (*Magn.* 14). To attain God—Ignatius also speaks of this wish in his other letters (*Eph.* 10.1; 12.2; *Trall.* 13.3; *Rom.* 1.1–2; 2.1). He sometimes also mentions "to attain Christ" (*Rom.* 5.3; 6.1); he wants to reach this goal with the help of friends' prayers. He believes that prayer completes him for God (*Phld.* 5.1). He asks to be prayed for in the name of Christ so that he may be found as God's sacrifice (*Rom.* 4.2). Through prayer he hopes to be blessed in Rome with martyrdom in the form of a fight with the animals (*Rom.* 1.2). "Ask only for power for me, both internal and external, so that I might not only speak but also desire, that I may not only be called a Christian but also be found (as such)" (*Rom.* 3.2). Ignatius has a burning wish to be allowed to prove himself as a true Christian, to be able to find his way into the fight, and to reach the way of sanctification as far as it is possible for a mere human. "But pray also for me because I need your love in God's mercy" (*Trall.* 12.3). Like Paul, Ignatius calls again and again on his friends and asks them for their prayer. He feels that he is weak and helpless. He knows that he needs as many true prayers as possible.

Ignatius particularly worries about his community. Through his death, it will remain without a guardian and caregiver.

---

94. von Loewenich, *Geschichte der Kirche*, 32–33.

"Consider the church in Syria in your prayer that has God for a shepherd in my place" (*Rom.* 9.1; similar exhortations to prayer for the church in Syria are in *Eph.* 21.2; *Trall.* 13.1; *Magn.* 14). How will it go for the community when their shepherd has been taken away? To be sure, God often has his own means and ways to care for his matters, but he demands of his faithful ones that they pray for one another and help one another.

The state of distress for the community in Syria should thus be considered as a common matter that concerns all. This distress must drive Christians who hear about it before God praying. Right belief and right love express themselves in the common bearing of burdens as a common cry to God for help. With these exhortations to supplicatory prayer, Ignatius probably wanted to nurture a common responsibility for the church and for the brothers. In this way, perhaps he also wanted to strengthen faith in himself as someone who prays, for faith remains living only through constant practice in prayer. Times of peace, security, and satiety are most dangerous for the believer.

Does God answer prayers? "I am still in danger, but the Father is faithful in Jesus Christ to fulfill my request and yours" (*Trall.* 13.3). "Since I have attained through my prayer to God to see your countenance that is worthy of God, as I have asked multiple times . . ." (*Rom.* 1.1). The former verse sounds like a liturgical formula and actually does not contain a personal share in the problem of answering prayer. It is different in the second verse. Here Ignatius says that God has answered his prayer to see his friends again. In general, one gains the impression that Ignatius was not occupied further with this problem. Answering prayer was probably an obvious matter for him. The Lord listens to the sighs of his faithful ones. One does not appeal to him in vain. However, as it stands, if God does not answer prayers, perhaps the opposite of what is asked for can happen? Struggles of faith and the questions of Job apparently did not concern Ignatius. To wrestle with them and suffer and finally still to trust God requires more than a life like that of Ignatius, which was short and full of eager expectation for the fulfillment of martyrdom.

Faith

Ignatius speaks only a little about the prayer of thanksgiving. A mention is found in *Smyrn.* 10.1. "They also thank the Lord for you because you have refreshed them in every way . . . ." The Christianity represented by Ignatius is defined in general by thankful joy. It is a life in which the view is forward-facing toward victory—a type of triumph in the middle of temporal hardships. Ignatius knows this, as his chains themselves shout to the community, "Remain in your harmony and in common prayer" (*Trall.* 12.2).

In terms of the importance of prayer, Ignatius differentiates various levels and possibilities. "For if the prayer of one or two has such power, how much more the prayer of the bishop and the entire church" (*Eph.* 5.2). If one person can already accomplish much with their prayers to God, the effectiveness multiplies itself in this way when there are many people praying. However, Ignatius considers the prayer of the bishop particularly effective. Is it perhaps also as effective as that of the community according to him? The words of the text can set up such a meaning. However, Ignatius probably does not intend to play the prayer of the bishop against the prayer of believers—both are equally effective and both are equally important before God. If Ignatius's words appear at first glance to arouse another impression, it should probably be attributed to the eagerness of his speech.

Ignatius represents a New Testament thought when he demands prayer both for friends and opponents. One should pray for them, although they are beasts in human form, that they might perhaps repent, which is certainly difficult (*Smyrn.* 4.1). "Pray also for other people[95] without ceasing" (*Eph.* 10.1). Even in this context, Ignatius points toward an anticipated repentance. One should counter the blasphemies of the opponents with prayers (*Eph.* 10.2). The spirit of the Sermon on the Mount becomes apparent in these words. Enemies should be treated with humility, friendliness, and modesty; evil should be paid back with good. The spirit of love, which can arise out of the Sermon on the Mount or can also come out of the Johannine legacy, is characteristic.

---

95. "The 'others' whom Ignatius mentions are non-Christians, in whom there is still 'hope for repentance'" (Grant, *Ignatius*, 41).

Faith and Love in Ignatius of Antioch

Faith and love acquiesce to unity in Ignatius's view of prayer. Faith manifests in prayer and is recognized through ἀγάπη toward the neighbor as well as to foreigners. This ἀγάπη does not discriminate between people because they originate from God. God's love is not selective but includes all creation without exception.

5. Faith and Justification

Expressions that concern the thought of justification are particularly seldom in Ignatius. The term itself only appears in two verses.

> Still, I am better educated by their abuse, but I am not justified (δεδικαίωμαι) by it (*Rom.* 5.1).

> But for me the archives are Jesus Christ, the holy archives are his cross, his death, his resurrection, and the faith that is established through him. Therein I want to be justified (δικαιωθῆναι) through your prayer (*Phld.* 8.2).

The almost complete lack of the concept of sin (ἁμαρτία) corresponds to the lack of the concept of justification (δικαιοσύνη).[96]

Molland represents the view that the Pauline concepts are applied in a false way in these verses.[97] The first of these two verses does not need to stand, however, absolutely in opposition to Pauline thoughts. Rather, a meeting point can be seen here in the thoughts of Ignatius and Paul. Ignatius thinks about the disciplining and refining effectiveness of suffering when he speaks of being better educated. However, this suffering has no salvation-historical or reconciling effectiveness before God—indeed that comes to expression here quite clearly. None of our deeds, not even martyrdom, helps us to redemption. The second verse is more difficult to interpret. How can one be justified through the prayer of others? Friends pray for salvation; God's mercy and these prayers accomplish the salvation of the sinner. First, Ignatius refers in this verse to Christ's cross, to his death, and to his resurrection as

---

96. Bultmann, "Ignatius und Paulus," 41.
97. Molland, "Heretics," 3.

Faith

objective actualities, then to faith as the subjective recipient of this gift of salvation. Although the concept of justification is obviously not used here in the Pauline sense, it can still be argued from the context that Ignatius also understood the justification of the sinner as God's work in Jesus Christ.

However, it must now be admitted that Ignatian thought on the question of justification does not employ Pauline terminology and also does not move along the same line, although Paul and Ignatius fundamentally mean the same thing. Ignatius has here contributed with this to creating the Eastern church's course. Although justification of Pauline character was not absolutely foreign to Eastern church piety, the theological reflection about the means and appropriation of salvation still went in other directions there by associating more with Johannine than Pauline notions.[98]

In Ignatian thought, one can already recognize the direction that the Eastern church will take. Redemption is not given so much through justification, but it is rather achieved as the person breaks away from the inclination to matter and from earthly bondage and is taken up into incorruptibility.[99] One speaks here of an actual mysticism for Ignatius and of its similar conception of salvation to the Eastern church.[100] Not the pursuit of justification but the desire for life dominates Ignatius's thought.[101] In the eyes of many scholars, Ignatian theology comes off badly in comparison with the New Testament. Indeed, it has not reached the Pauline depth, particularly in the question of justification. However, too strict a benchmark is still laid here, and Ignatian theology is not considered as a whole.[102] Ignatius probably knew the Pauline thoughts

---

98. Joest, "Rechtfertigung," 828.

99. Schlier, *Religionsgeschichtliche Untersuchungen*, 179.

100. von der Goltz, *Ignatius*, 112.

101. Bultmann, "Ignatius und Paulus," 42.

102. Riesenfeld criticizes Bultmann's view in this respect. "But in fact no comparisons of this kind ought to be carried out without putting the question whether, in view of the historical setting of Paul on the one hand and of Ignatius on the other, the latter was able, in his time and in his milieu, to understand the struggle of Paul the Jew in solving the predominant problems of Jewish religion, such as law and righteousness, and fully to evaluate Paul's definition

Faith and Love in Ignatius of Antioch

in chapters 5–8 of Romans about Christ as victor over the corruptive powers of hate, sin, law, and death. The bishop of Antioch has placed the emphasis on the last point, namely, on the victory over the powers of death (cf. φάρμακον ἀθανασίας [*Eph.* 20.2]). Although Ignatius has not developed these thoughts further, he belongs to the representatives of the classical (classical-dramatic) doctrine of reconciliation—that formed a line at the time of the early church from the New Testament to Irenaeus, Origen, and Athanasius, and on to Basil the Great.

Meinhold has determined, to recapitulate, that the concept of faith in Ignatius's theological thought is not related to the difficult problem of the doctrine of justification, as is the case with Paul, or to the questions that arise from the relationship of sin and grace. These occupy only a very small space in his theology. For Ignatius, Christ has not released people from the curse of sin that increases through the law but rather redeems them from perishability as he has brought the new, imperishable, godly life victoriously into the world through his death.[103]

Ignatius does not, therefore, fundamentally represent a different line from Paul. He has only put the accents otherwise in the treatment of the salvific event. He places the main emphasis on Christology. Since questions precisely about Christology were hotly contested at this time, soteriology was pushed somewhat in the shadows as a result. Christ was true God and true human, and, as such, he became our brother and Redeemer. Faith in him rescues. "Judgment comes also on heavenly powers if they do not believe on Christ's blood" (*Smyrn.* 6.1). If Christ has truly suffered and died, salvation lies in faith in him alone. Rüsch has rightly observed that Ignatius lies far from any consideration of merit. He knows that Christ's suffering is a gift of grace about which no

---

of the salvation conceived as liberation from bondage of law and establishment of a new righteousness. On the contrary it seems, in a historical perspective, quite natural that Ignatius would be concerned above all with what was the crucial problem of the Greek mind in his time, the experience of destruction and death and the longing for an imperishable life" ("Reflections," 318–19).

103. Meinhold, "Ethik," 54.

Faith

person can boast before God as if it is their own merit.[104] Both Paul and Ignatius see salvation in the reconciling work of Jesus Christ alone. Participation in that through meritorious work from the person's side is excluded. However, Paul highlights that to a far greater degree than Ignatius and with repeated, strong emphasis.

Can one speak of a "justification by faith" in Ignatius? Although the material is scarce in this respect, this question should be answered in the affirmative. Admittedly, Ignatius does not use the same terminology as Paul, yet, as has been shown, he is on about the same thing.

How is the sinful person reconciled with God? How are they made pleasing to him? The answer is the same in Paul as in Ignatius. Nothing that the person can bring before God is suitable as the basis for redemption. To speak with Luther, a *iustitia aliena* is necessary regarding this—a justification that is given to people through Christ. Anders Nygren observes that Pauline thought about the ἀγάπη of the cross is a living reality for Ignatius.[105] Only God's incomprehensible love brings us salvation, a love that expresses itself most clearly in that he has given his own Son for all, even for enemies.

Ignatius speaks particularly often about God's grace. "Farewell in God's grace" (*Smyrn.* 13.2). "The grace of God will repay him in every way" (*Smyrn.* 12.1). "For I trust in grace" (*Pol.* 7.2; cf. *Smyrn.* 9.2; *Pol.* 1.2). "I trust in the grace of Jesus Christ that will release every bond from you" (*Phld.* 8.1). "But may those who mistreated them find forgiveness in the grace of Jesus Christ" (*Phld.* 11.1). Above all, God's grace expresses itself in the suffering and death of Jesus Christ.[106]

Grace is essentially a soteriological word, as Corwin says. However, the expression used by her is too weak if what is meant by that is only that grace is a divine help for people to their rescue.[107] Grace signifies a gift without any merit for Ignatius; it alone

---

104. Rüsch, *Entstehung*, 74.
105. Nygren, *Den kristna kärlekstanken*, 2.42.
106. Grant, *Ignatius*, 136.
107. "Grace is thus essentially a soteriological word, for it means the divine

makes salvation possible. It is not only a help that one can perhaps also do without or a first impetus in an otherwise also successful act of salvation. In a similar way, Torrance assesses the concept of grace in Ignatius too weakly when he sees in it only a completing factor in the event of salvation.[108]

In the center of Ignatius's collective religious-theological worldview is the notion of God's economy (οἰκονομία) in the world. He wants to release the world and humanity from the violence of the ruler of this world. In Jesus Christ, God's Son, God appeared on earth for the revelation of new, eternal life.[109] If Ignatius's Christianity is recognized as mysticism, then it is a Christian mysticism through and through that is grounded on the incarnation and reconciliation through Jesus Christ.[110] The thought of justification can still be added to these two points. Jesus Christ, true God and true human, has reconciled us through his suffering, his death, and his resurrection. We are redeemed through faith in his blood. Therein lies our justification before God.

---

help extended to men for their salvation" (Corwin, *St. Ignatius*, 164).

108. "χάρις is the principle or potency emanating from God which it is necessary to obtain if the believer is to attain at last to the divine μέγεθος and complete union with God. . . . Our part is to see to our unity, in faith and love; χάρις which completes our salvation by uniting us to the fullness of God is a divine gift to those who are worthy" (Torrance, *Doctrine of Grace*, 83).

109. Krüger, "Briefe des Ignatius," 520.

110. Tinsley, "Imitatio Christi," 554.

3

Love

1. Martyrdom as an Expression of Love for Jesus

For Ignatius the martyr-bishop, Jesus Christ stands in the center of his life, thought, feeling, and pursuit (*Eph.* 11.1; *Rom.* 5.3)—this Rackl rightly recognized.[1] Inner love for Christ is evident in the attempt to be his true disciple. "Be imitators (μιμηταί) of Jesus Christ" (*Phld.* 7.2; cf. *Magn.* 9.2; *Eph.* 1.1, 3; *Trall.* 1.2). "Allow me to be an imitator of the suffering of my God" (*Rom.* 6.3). What the essential part of being a disciple is for Ignatius proceeds from this last mentioned verse. It is necessary above all to follow the master on the path of suffering. We encounter here the thought of martyrdom. It is striking that the concept of witness (μάρτυς) is missing in Ignatius. The bishop of Antioch obviously did not know it.[2] The idea of martyrdom and the ancient concepts of

---

1. Rackl, *Christologie*, 4. "Wie eine brennende Fakkel leuchtet seine Liebe zu Christus durch die Jahrhunderte" (von Loewenich, *Geschichte der Kirche*, 29).

2. von Campenhausen, *Die Idee des Martyriums*, 52. In the author's opinion, the use of John's Gospel and direct Johannine thought in Ignatius

μαρτυρία, μάρτυς, and μαρτυρεῖν go back to the John the apostle and Evangelist.[3]

During a persecution of Christians in Antioch, Ignatius was arrested, condemned, and sent to Rome where he met death by wild beasts in the arena. The persecution came about because the first Christians were made responsible for an earthquake—for an earthquake that Malas called θεομηνία, "sign of divine wrath."[4]

If one does not count Paul, Ignatius is the first Christian martyr about whose personal disposition we are taught.[5] Ignatius's statement about this is extensive and thorough. It shows an image of a man whose burning wish is martyrdom, who hopes for that, asks for that, and always speaks about it in his letters.

> But why then have I handed myself over to death, to fire, to sword, to beasts? To be near the sword is to be near to God; to be in the presence of beasts is to be in the presence of God—so long as it is in the name of Jesus Christ! I endure everything to suffer with him, if he, the one who became perfect human, might strengthen me (*Smyrn.* 4.2).

Apocryphal fragments could stand behind these words, such as the following words cited in the *Gospel of Thomas* as the words of Jesus: "Whoever is near to me is near to the fire; whoever is far from me is far from the kingdom" (similarly in a Greek proverb: the one who is near to Zeus is near to the light). If Ignatius knew these words, he has changed the word order and reversed the meaning.[6] He wants to depict the endurance of dangers and the suffering of martyrdom as a thing that is particularly pleasing to God. Reminiscences of the motif of God's hiddenness can also be discerned in this verse as similarly in Ps 23 ("And even if I walk through the dark valley, I fear no evil. For you are with me; your

---

cannot be verified (ibid., 52n.8). Von der Goltz already compiled a table that shows many Ignatian expressions are actually Johannine (*Ignatius*, 196–203).

3. von Campenhausen, *Die Idee des Martyriums*, 55.
4. Downey, *History*, 215.
5. von Campenhausen, *Die Idee des Martyriums*, 67.
6. Grant, *Ignatius*, 117.

Love

rod and your staff comfort me"), and they are also found in the Sermon on the Mount. A person's life and security always lie in the hand of the heavenly Father, particularly when they are surrounded by hardships and dangers. Here it is true that whoever is near to God can never really have need.

In Ignatius's opinion, the way of martyrdom has its beginning in the Old Testament. The prophets who were near to God have already lived like Jesus Christ. Like him, they were persecuted (*Magn.* 8.2; cf. Matt 5:11–12; Luke 11:47–51; Acts 7:51–52). Ignatius here falls into line with the New Testament tradition that brings the persecution of the prophets in connection with suffering for the sake of Christ.[7]

In his letter to the Roman community, Ignatius describes how he has fought with beasts from Syria to Rome, on water and on land, by day and by night. He feels like he is bound to ten leopards. (He means the division of soldiers who have to guard him on the way.) These only become more severe with the good deeds that their prisoner bestows on them (*Rom.* 5.1). Because the image of leopards is encountered here for the first time in Greco-Roman literature,[8] it was probably devised by Ignatius himself. This beast is well-known to be particularly wild and dangerous. This comparison should illustrate in what a difficult situation Ignatius found himself as a prisoner between the coarse soldiers.

Ignatius contents himself in this depiction of his experiences with a pompous "royal" style (regal-imperial style).[9] One is tempted to ask whether the depiction is not generously exaggerated. Ignatius probably wants here at this moment to paint the triumph of martyrdom with particularly glowing and impressive colors.

Ignatius is compelled by a burning wish to be able to suffer martyrdom. He is so obsessed by it that he worries whether he will reach his goal. He has heard that the beasts do not always attack

---

7. Cf. ibid., 62.
8. Fischer, *Die apostolischen Väter*, 187.
9. Grant, *Ignatius*, 90.

those who are chosen as sacrifices.¹⁰ Therefore, if the beasts do not seize him voluntarily, he wants to help by force (*Rom.* 5.2). Ignatius means that, although he considers himself as last among the believers, he has been counted worthy of God's honor to have been found as a sacrifice (*Eph.* 21.2). This sacrifice is now brought on the way of martyrdom. He is finally to reach his goal by this, and he wishes that he will not be found to be useless (*Trall.* 12.3). Regarding this, Bauer remarks that there were Christians from the beginning who have directed the attention of the authority on themselves in order to gain the crown of martyrdom through this. Bauer cites a number of texts that tell of such attempts.¹¹ To be a martyr was afterward the highest and most worthwhile thing in life for many Christians. What becomes of the preaching of the gospel if all would choose the fate of a martyr? Who would put down a witness for Christ and carry further the good news? We do not know how Ignatius solved this problem. Perhaps Ignatius was not really concerned with this question any further. His view was probably that he personally was called to be a martyr but that not everyone was thus required along this path and that it was not mandatory for all. Von Campenhausen indicates that, in all the pathos and deliberate solemnity of his language in the Ignatian letters, still no place can be found that was merely rhetorical or conventional.¹² However, his burning zeal and his flowing style allow the question about whether martyrdom is not depicted by him in overly rosy colors, whether here the suffering and hardship are not idealized too much. Yet one must consider Ignatius's personality and the time in which he lived. Ignatius was wholeheartedly a Christian. With everything in him, he wanted to serve the Lord without holding back—even the commitment of his life did not appear to be too much to him. Rather, in his view, martyrdom was the consummate possibility for such a complete commitment.

Friends probably wanted to deter the bishop from going on this path to martyrdom. For Ignatius, however, it was an

10. Ibid., 91.
11. Bauer, *Briefe*, 247.
12. von Campenhausen, *Die Idee des Martyriums*, 68–69.

undeserved gift of grace that his burning wish should come true. "Therefore, I am afraid of your love, that it might harm me" (*Rom.* 1.2). Ignatius does not want the Roman Christians to come to help him in alleged care at the wrong time. "Let me be food for the beasts through whom it is possible to attain God. I am God's wheat, and I am ground by the teeth of the beasts so that I may be found as the pure bread of Christ. Rather, coax the beasts that they may become a grave for me and leave no part of my body behind so that I may not become a burden to anyone after death" (*Rom.* 4.1-2). For the notion of "pure bread," history-of-religions parallels can be found, for instance, in the food offerings of the Jews. In the preparation of this food offering, it was necessary to consider outward purity. This applied both to the meal and to other ingredients as well as to the manner of production. Nothing could be left over for the next morning (see, for instance, Mal 1:11). The same language and image as in Ignatius can be found in the description that Josephus gives of these sacrifices.[13] Similarly, as in this cultic action of Judaism in which one must observe outer purity and completely use the bread so that no remainder was left, so also the corpse of the martyr, who used his life as a sacrifice for God, should disappear completely. Perhaps still closer is the thought about the bread of Holy Communion that indeed corresponds to the unleavened bread of the Jewish Passover festival.[14] In any case, a connection between the celebration of the Eucharist and martyrdom should not be overlooked.[15] Yet perhaps an even more distant thought comes into the picture when Ignatius says that his corpse should disappear entirely. In this, he also wants to be an imitator of Jesus Christ, whose grave was certainly empty on Easter morning and whose corpse disappeared (cf. *Rom.* 4.1-2).

---

13. Lightfoot, *Apostolic Fathers*, 2.2.207.

14. Grant, *Ignatius*, 89.

15. "Der Parallelismus zwischen Eucharistie und Martyriums ist offensichtlich. Beide aktualisieren in der Darbringung des Kreuzes—bzw. Lebensopfers an den Vater im Hl. Geist im Grund das nähmliche Heilsgeheimnis" (Hamman, "Trinität," 2.141).

Ignatius brings the thought of sacrifice to expression in *Rom.* 2.2 more clearly than in *Rom.* 4.1–2, the verse mentioned above. "Grant me nothing more than to be sacrificed to God while an altar is still prepared so that you may form a choir in love and can sing praise to the Father in Christ Jesus because God has counted the bishop of Syria worthy to be found in the region of the setting sun after sending him from its rising" (*Rom.* 2.2). Ignatius looks at martyrdom as a sacrificial action in which he is present with the community.[16] He clearly is thinking here about the Amphitheatrum Flavium, the later Colosseum, where he should face death. It was built for animal and gladiator fights, but for Christians it was connected to the memory of martyrs. Ignatius now calls the arena in this amphitheater an altar around which the Roman Christians have gathered and sing a hymn of sacrifice for the heavenly Father.[17] With the image of the sunset and sunrise, Ignatius probably wants to recall his own life, whose beginning and end stand under God's protection in all shifting dangers.

Regarding his martyrdom, Ignatius says that he scarcely ever will have the opportunity to attain God if the recipients of his letter are not silent about him (*Rom.* 2.1). That means that they should take absolutely no measures to stop the enforcement of the verdict on Ignatius. In the same context, Ignatius indicates that a better opportunity will never be provided for the Roman Christians themselves to associate their names with a good work. According to Fischer, Ignatius pictures his martyrdom here as a work of art that the community in Rome can sign with their names, provided they do not take it upon themselves to rescue him.[18] "My spirit is dedicated for you not only now but also when I attain God. For I am still in danger, but the Father is faithful in Jesus Christ to fulfill my request and yours. May you be found blameless in him" (*Trall.*

---

16. von Campenhausen, *Die Idee des Martyriums*, 72.

17. Grant, *Ignatius*, 87. Grant also points to Lightfoot, who brings parallels to the sacrificial altar: θυσιαστήριον=Amphitheatrum Flavium. Cf. *Eph.* 8.1 and its interpretation in ibid., 39–40.

18. Fischer, *Die apostolischen Väter*, 185.

13.3). A possible staying of martyrdom is meant by the danger about which Ignatius speaks.[19]

Paul urges the Romans to present their bodies as a sacrifice that is living, holy, and pleasing to God (Rom 12:1). We have no certainty about whether Ignatius knew this word of Paul. The content of this thought, however, is also found in him and, what is more, in a rigorously heightened form. The sacrifice that belongs to every type of cult since time immemorial is the first and most important concept in Ignatius's "ethic." For him there is no relationship to God without the sacrifice's deep earnestness.[20] Paul wants in this verse to express that believing persons should give themselves to Christ himself as a thank offering so that their lives will be sanctified.[21] This view also appears in Ignatius. Yet he has thought it through to its most extreme end and has reached a conclusion with which Paul probably would no longer agree entirely. According to Paul, full devotion to God means that the person can be led from above in everything that they do. Ignatius wants this leading to be understood teleologically, to a goal, namely, to martyrdom. Here alone can the believer show a true sense of sacrifice through the unconditional commitment of body and soul to the Lord. However, the question is raised here whether the almost-overstated, active willingness with which the body is overcome by wrenching beasts is not influenced by gnostic thought. According to that, the body is in itself bad and worthless because it consists of corruptible material that must be shed. Ignatius does not base the value of martyrdom on such views, but these notions may have still influenced his thought. The thought of von Loewenich is that a foreign and unbiblical spirit has crept into Ignatius's worldviews despite all the love for Christ. Greek thought, which is defined by dualism between spirit and material, allows him to praise Holy Communion as the conquest of corporeality and as "the medicine of incorporeality."[22] The same spirit could stand behind his

---

19. Grant, *Ignatius*, 81.
20. Althaus, *Der Brief an die Römer*, 106.
21. Gulin, *Roomalaiskirje*, 166.
22. von Loewenich, *Geschichte der Kirche*, 29–30.

striving for martyrdom and behind his wish that his body may be consumed. How far Greco-gnostic notions come into play with individual Christian notions cannot always be clearly differentiated in Ignatius's thought about martyrdom. It also remains questionable to what extent it is necessary to reckon with Jewish influence in this context. Few conspicuous echoes of the Old Testament are found in Ignatius; indeed, he sometimes even speaks negatively about Judaism. He considers it to be old leaven that one must avoid and flee. In the context of martyrdom, however, the question is raised about whether or not the Jewish Pentecost provision and the command to leave nothing remaining from the bread of the food offering have influenced Ignatius when he wishes for the complete consumption of his body.

If Ignatius hopes to partake of the animal fights through the prayer of the community in Rome, it is also his wish to be able to prove himself as a true disciple of Jesus through it (*Eph.* 1.2). The sense of martyrdom is summarized briefly and clearly here. It is the realization of discipleship through carrying the cross. The following of Jesus Christ's disciples is then only complete when they are crowned through martyrdom[23] and involves a self-sacrifice of witness (μάρτυς!). The baptized believer whose blood has not yet flowed for the confession of his Lord is only a beginner in discipleship. They cannot yet raise a claim to the label of true disciple.[24]

How did Ignatius picture the way of a "normal" disciple? Indeed, all cannot go on the way of martyrdom, and the cross cannot be equally heavy for all. On Ignatius's view, can a Christian, who does not have to suffer for the confession of the name of Christ, really be called a true disciple of Jesus? This question can probably still be affirmed, for, in his letters, Ignatius has primarily described his own way, to which the martyr's death belongs indivisibly. However, he does not demand the same of others—God's will and God's plan are not the same for all Christians![25] Ignatius's view on

23. Lightfoot, *Apostolic Fathers*, 2.2.31.
24. Bauer, *Briefe*, 198.
25. Richardson writes, "It must be noted, however, that Ignatius does not urge all men to become martyrs. While he conceives of martyrdom as

this question can be summarized in the following way. The way that leads to God with certainty is that of the cross and suffering; it is the way on which Christ, the master, has already gone ahead himself. It is noteworthy that Ignatius does not invoke the words of Jesus himself in this context.

Ignatius was obviously of the view that martyrs are indispensable for Christianity. They show clearly and distinctly which victims among believers claim a true discipleship of Christ. The "ordinary" Christians will witness the martyr's fate. They will struggle together, suffer together, and rejoice together. They will form the "choir" that exalts the triumph of the one who dies for Christ.

It can now be asked at this point whether or not Ignatius has destroyed unity in the life of the Christian community through this difference between martyrs, on the one hand, and the choir of "ordinary" Christians, on the other. Indeed, otherwise he always emphasizes this unity. Yet when martyrdom comes up for discussion, he suddenly appears to see a difference and to play a "higher" way of life off of a "lower" way of life. Perhaps through this Ignatius offered the first impulse for the development that led to the emergence of two different ideals of life in the Catholic Church. Consequently, the formulation of a particular spiritual "status" followed from these first attempts, to which the martyrs initially belonged, and later the ecclesial ascetics, spirituals, monks, and nuns. Beside this, then, there was the second, lower status of simple believers, the lay Christians.[26] Here it can be revealed how the ideal of discipleship has changed over the course of time. In the New Testament, above all in the Synoptics, the right follower of Jesus is the disciple. In the Apostolic Fathers, above all in Ignatius,

---

the means whereby he himself will gain the true life, he does not expressly state that this is the only way to attain salvation. Others may reach the divine through their own particular sufferings, which do not necessarily include martyrdom (*Smyrn.* 9.2). The will of God may not be the same for all believers" (*Christianity*, 24).

26. Schlier, *Religionsgeschichtliche Untersuchungen*, 179. In Ignatius "die Nachahmung Christi durch das Gleichwerden mit dem Herrn im Martyrium zur Vollendung geführt" (Adam, "Mystik," 1246).

Faith and Love in Ignatius of Antioch

it is the martyrs. In the Middle Ages, it is the monk. And finally in Lutheran Christianity, it is the mature layperson.[27]

Suffering belongs indivisibly to following Christ. History-of-religions comparative material can be found in all times for the relationship of suffering as a way to unification with divinity. Schlier studied this concept in Ignatius as well as the mystics and determined that a certain boundary was maintained by Ignatius even in the language with regard to the unification of the redeemer and the martyr. It does not express the identity of both but only a μιμεῖσθαι of the martyr or initiate.[28] Campenhausen emphasized that Ignatius did not use the concept of μίμησις precisely in the questionable cultic-mystical sense.[29] Jesus's suffering always remains the central point[30] even when Ignatius draws in many places on the language of mystery cults as, for example, in *Eph.* 12.2: You are a passageway for those slain for God, fellow initiates (συμμύσται) of Paul, the holy one, who received testimony, and was worthy of blessing. The last part indicates the connection of the Ephesians to Paul. An example of this is also recounted in Acts 20:18.[31]

If Ignatius emphasizes martyrdom so strongly, then the question arises whether he attached salvific importance to it. Thoughts along this line have been variously expressed.[32] Upon closer inspection, it clearly appears that Ignatius differentiates between Christ's suffering and the martyrs' suffering. The former accom-

---

27. Tarvainen, "Apostolisten isien käsitys Kristuksen seuraamisesta," 334.

28. Schlier, *Religionsgeschichtliche Untersuchungen*, 164.

29. von Campenhausen, *Die Idee des Martyriums*, 77. The author points to the studies of Richard Reitzenstein and Gillis Petersson Wetter, in which the significance of the history-of-religions material is exaggerated in his view. On this, compare also Bartsch, *Gnostische Gut*, 90.

30. von Campenhausen, *Die Idee des Martyriums*, 75n.1

31. Lightfoot, *Apostolic Fathers*, 2.2.63.

32. "Dem verstärkten Einfluss des gnostischen Erlösungsmythos und griechischer Unsterblichkeitssehnsucht bei Ignatius entsprach die Einschränkung der eschatologischen Zukunft auf das Martyrium als Erlösung und die Betonung ihrer Gegenwart in einer sakramentalen Christusexistenz" (Andresen, "Erlösung," 2.590).

plishes salvation alone, while the latter must be understood as a sacrificial service that is necessary to accomplish with a grateful heart, that has no soteriological significance, and that also may not lead to pride or boasting. However, in martyrdom Ignatius catches sight of a type of certainty that one is situated on the right way. At this point he differentiates himself from Paul, for whom there is no such certainty or such assurance about salvation.[33]

In one respect, however, a connection persists between Christ's suffering and the martyr's suffering. "For if this was accomplished by our Lord in appearance, then I am likewise bound in appearance" (*Smyrn.* 4.2). These words are directed against representatives of the docetic view. They say, "If Christ did not really suffer, then we also cannot suffer with him." Here again it appears that Ignatius's entire theology is Christology at its base. Even the question of martyrdom leads finally to the question of Christ. The reality of Christ and that of his followers correspond to one another. They cannot be considered without one another. The docetic Christ cannot bring redemption. The Christ who lived, suffered, died, and was raised for us as true human and true God is alone the ground of our salvation.

Traits are found in the person of Ignatius that appear to stand in contradiction. On the one hand, he is a farsighted ecclesial leader, who recognizes and calls for the importance of office, doctrine, and order in the community. On the other hand, there is only one important thing for him in his unconditional and enthusiastic commitment, namely, to prove his ardent love for the Lord through martyrdom. However, one can ask here whether a statement is not also contained in this as regards the right doctrine. Thus Adalbert Hamman sees in Ignatius's martyrdom something like a confession of the Trinity, of faith in God the Father, Son,

---

33. "Unpaulinisch ist allerdings, dass Ign. im Märtyrertode gleichsam eine Garantie sieht, dass er ihn nicht einfach als vom Herrn gefügt hinnimmt, sondern aus dem Todesgeschick nun noch gleichsam ein Werk macht, das ihm Sicherheit gibt und dass er deshalb die römische Gemeinde bestürmt, seinen Märtyrertod nicht zu verhindern" (Bultmann, "Ignatius und Paulus," 50).

and Holy Spirit.[34] Such an interpretation would lend the life of the bishop of Antioch and his end a still deeper meaning.

2. The Humility that Love Effects

Love effects not only a preparation to suffer for the sake of Christ but also humility. Thus, for example, Ignatius can write to the Ephesians:

> Whoever does not appear at the gathering is already owned by pride and has judged himself. For it is written, "God opposes the proud" (*Eph.* 5.3).

Love, therefore, does not make a person bigger, and it also does not emphasize them among others. To the contrary, it lowers them. Ignatius appeals to biblical expressions. Both the Old Testament (e.g., Prov 3:34) and also the New Testament (e.g., Jas 4:6; 1 Pet 5:5) speak about God opposing the proud. Where Ignatius has specifically obtained this thought, we do not know. This word was obviously one of the basic truths at the time of early Christianity that have been emphasized both in proclamation as well as in doctrine. One has glimpsed the primal sin in pride. It is the ancient aspiration of the person to get to the same level with God (*eritis sicut Deus!*). It is the wrong estimate of one's own place. It is the pull toward unilateral action and self-rule that does not want to give honor to God.

The one who pulls away from the community is owned by pride in Ignatius's view. Such a person supposes that they can come out alone and do not need the community in the worship service or in Holy Communion. They consider themselves to be able to eschew the support of other believers. They thus reject all the things that the Lord has given to his own as help so that they remain consistent in faith. They suppose that they no longer belong to the

---

34. "So erweist sich auch das Zeugnis der Märtyrer als ein Bekenntnis zur Trinität. Die Ignatiusbriefe, aber auch die Märtyrerakten belegen dies deutlich" (Hamman, "Trinität," 2.141). Cf. Scheffczyk, "Das Werden des Trinitätsdogmas," 151.

weak who require such help. They imagine themselves strong, yet they cheat themselves and have already pronounced their own verdict on themselves. Right love humbles and demonstrates to one that they need the community of believers. However, pride blinds so that one separates oneself from the *communio* and considers oneself to be able to find their way alone.

The fact of Ignatius's humble attitude shows that he himself admits he is susceptible to the temptations of pride. "I think many things in God, but I take measure of myself so that I may not go to destruction for boastfulness. For now I must fear all the more and may not listen to those who could make me proud. For those who speak to me flog me" (*Trall.* 4.1). The fearless bishop who went to meet death had many admirers who freely expressed their feelings and praised his courage, his determination, and his other gifts. How far these expressions were honorably meant and did not only want to flatter cannot be decided. In any case, for Ignatius they brought the temptation of pride with them. Ignatius indicates this danger in candid self-examination. He knows that he suffers shipwreck in faith and in discipleship if he gives in to this temptation. Therefore, he is strong and candid in front of his friends. His words recall the chiding words that Jesus directed toward Peter. "Get behind me Satan! You are a scandal to me, for you do not think what is godly but what is human" (Matt 16:23). Ignatius warns the Magnesians that they should not get caught on the fishhooks of a delusion (*Magn.* 11.1). He says that the bishop has not obtained the service to the community from himself or through people but through the love of God the Father and the Lord Jesus Christ (*Phld.* 1.1). Later, pride would be counted as a deadly sin (*peccata mortalia*) in the church; the *tentatio vanae gloriae* is a well-known temptation of the pious warriors of the faith from the Middle Ages. Ignatius probably has played a part in continuing to steer the development of the concept of sin in this direction. Although he initially influenced the Eastern church above all, he has still influenced the evolution of doctrine in the Western church.

However, not only fame and honor could dissuade a Christian from the right way. Temptations also approached those who

Faith and Love in Ignatius of Antioch

are called through the development of stronger offices in the community. "Let a position not make anyone prideful, for all is faith and love, than which nothing is greater" (*Smyrn.* 6.1). As was already mentioned above (p. 1–2), Ignatius probably refers to deacons and presbyters with this reproof. Later the canons of the councils of Nicaea (Canons 18–19) and Chalcedon (Canon 15), in whose power struggles boundaries are set for deacons and deaconesses, show that this question always presented a reemerging and periodically quite difficult inward problem for the church in ancient time. When Ignatius urges a consolidation of ecclesial office, he does not want to create a self-consciously hierarchical state. Rather, he wants to give servants and leaders to the community who are permeated by love and are always there for believers. As pride signifies one of the greatest dangers for those who occupy any societal position, so it is also one of the most difficult temptations in the spiritual life. It belongs to the "sins of the spirit" that are not able to be recognized easily and that nevertheless, or even precisely for this reason, are able to inflict heavy damage on the kingdom of God. Human nature is ready at any time to capitulate to pride and to make use of all honor for itself. A particular office and a high place tempts particularly easily to this sin. However, when the guiding stars for every act are faith and love, then the danger of pride can be circumvented, or at least recognized at the right time so that one can fight back against it.

Ignatius knows this struggle from his own experience. He knows how quickly a person can be disarmed and how easily they surrender faintheartedly. Neither the office nor the way of martyrdom protect against such defeats—even a bishop like Ignatius always has to begin from scratch in discipleship. "Now I am beginning to be a disciple" (*Rom.* 5.3). "I am not yet a disciple" (*Trall.* 5.2). "For I have needed to be anointed by you with faith, admonition, patience, and steadfastness" (*Eph.* 3.1).

Ignatius considers himself as one of the last among believers. He is first a beginner in the struggle of faith. He means that he has hardly reached the place of a disciple. Was that really humility or hidden pride? Is it that Ignatius speaks so disparagingly of himself that pastoral wisdom is perhaps hidden? Perhaps Ignatius wants to nurture his community to patience with these words, in which he shows them that even a bishop is a person fraught with errors and is first a beginner in discipleship. If the Ephesians test themselves subsequently, they will determine that it is ordered no differently with them and that they have no occasion to think something great of themselves. Their eyes have been opened, and they will lead in modesty and humility—so Ignatius probably hopes. Ignatius here thinks of the exhortation of the apostle Paul. One should consider "the other as higher than oneself in humility" (Phil 2:3).

Thus Ignatius writes, "Pray for the church in Syria, from which I am led in chains to Rome as the least of those who believe there, as I was counted worthy to be found for God's honor" (*Eph.* 21.2). "For I am likewise not worthy, as the least of them and a miscarriage" (*Rom.* 9.2). Ignatius used the word ἔσχατος, while Paul indicated in 1 Cor 15:9 that he is the least of the apostles (ἐλάχιστος τῶν ἀποστόλων; cf. *Magn.* 14.1; *Smyrn.* 11.1). Corwin intends to make the failings that Ignatius experienced and the losses that he suffered responsible for this deep humility of his. It thus concerns not so much the persecutions that have made the bishop of Antioch so humble but rather an inner crisis that is responsible for a schism in the community.[35] Harrison also represents a similar view.[36]

The hypothesis of Corwin and Harrison may be reasonable, but it cannot be verified through historical facts. It depends only on suppositions. It then makes the issue with Ignatius not chiefly about actual humility but about shame over himself and perhaps also about an ironic attitude toward his own failure and the fiascoes in the care for the office.

It would probably have still been the case that Ignatius experienced difficulties and disappointments as bishop, but that these would hardly have been able to have influenced his basic attitude toward the question of humility. It appears most credible that the severity of the last struggle and the expectation of death moved

---

35. Corwin, *St. Ignatius*, 27–29; cf. Grant, *Ignatius*, 54.
36. Harrison, *Polycarp's Two Epistles*, 79–106.

this question into the foreground so strongly for him. Faith and love do not exalt a person, but they teach them the proper self-assessment and show that the correct place for a Christian is the place under the last and the least of the brothers. Ignatius has gone down the same road as Paul already before him, whose thoughts were well-known to him.

If the Ignatian sayings here display a significant connection with Pauline sayings, it could then be asked whether Ignatius was, like Paul, first an enemy and persecutor of Jesus Christ's community who later found the way to Christianity. This problem remains unresolved because the sources do not offer information.

"I am not enjoining you like Peter and Paul. They were apostles; I am a convict. They were free; I am now a slave" (*Rom.* 4.3). Ignatius could have the report about the martyrdom of Peter and Paul, the "princes of the apostles," in Rome from *1 Clem.* 5 or from other sources.[37] Ignatius here compares himself with these two men and demonstrates thereby that he is a person who does not have a wish remaining. He has obtained a frame of mind that is considered the classic Cynic-Stoic ideal.[38] This ideal of "serenity," this giving up of all wishes, is not particularly Christian. It is primarily the way of mystics and not the way of personal-ethical faith.

Ignatius writes to the community in Smyrna that he is not worthy of his local origin because he is the least among them (11.1). In a similar way, he formulates the same thought with respect to the community in Syria (*Trall.* 13.1). He says to the Ephesians that he is the last of their servants (*Eph.* 8.1)[39] and wishes to be found as their disciple in the resurrection (*Pol.* 6.1). In all these places, the humility that is characteristic for Ignatius comes to expression.

---

37. Fischer, *Die apostolischen Väter*, 187.

38. Grant, *Ignatius*, 90.

39. Fischer translates the word περίψημα with the word "Sühnopfer" (*Die apostolischen Väter*, 149) and Grant with the word "sacrifice" (*Ignatius*, 40). The translations of Andrén ("eder ringe tjänare"; *Apostoliska fäderna*, 63) and Stenroth ("kaikkein halvin palvelijanne"; i.e., the last of all you servants; *Apostolisten isien kirjat*, 41) seem most accurate. The word περίψημα appears in Paul: we have become as the scum of the earth (1 Cor 4:13).

However, here also opposing traits can be recognized in Ignatius in a similar way as in the question about martyrdom. On the one hand, he emphasizes the significance and dignity of the episcopacy in nothing less than an extreme manner. On the other hand, he places himself, the bishop of Antioch, in the last place in the community. The order in the church and the office that he occupies raise him to the highest place in the community. However, love lowers him to the least among believers and makes him the humble servant of all.

Ignatius has imparted the heritage of the biblical thought of *humilitas* into the next century. God opposes the proud. To be the last and the least is the right attitude for the Christian. That also appears when Gregory the Great assumes the title *servus servorum Dei* (cf. Leo the Great: *servitus*; Justinian: *ultimus servus minimus*). Quite similarly, Martin Luther emphasizes the thought of *humilitas* at a later time. It is interesting to note that the thought of humility is expressed again and again in Finnish Christianity as in Ignatius, particularly in many songs. There it is humbly prayed that the Redeemer might make us to be his disciples. It is said that we are only weak beginners who hope that God will recognize one who stands in the lowest place as his own. The recognition of the greatness and holiness of God presses a person down and makes them holy—this experience is common to Christians at all times.

3. Mutual Love

Faith and love go hand in hand on Ignatius's view. They stand in close relationship. Sometimes he considers both of these concepts, but he also does so individually. For example, he speaks in the following verses only about love. He greets the love of the brothers at Troas (*Phld.* 11.2). His spirit greets the love of the churches (*Rom.* 9.3). He tells of well-ordered, godly love (*Magn.* 1.1). In these expressions, both Johannine and Pauline notions of love are reflected. God is love—let us love because he first loved us—the love between Paul and the communities—points of contact are found in the thought of both apostles.

How is the thought of love achieved in peoples' common life? Ignatius has repeatedly contemplated this. For example, the attitude toward slavery was a touchstone of the old world for love of neighbor.

> "Do not treat male and female slaves proudly. However, they should also not puff themselves up, but they should still be slaves even more for the glory of God in order that they may gain a greater freedom from God. They should not long to be free at the community's cost, lest they be found slaves of desire" (*Pol.* 4.3).

Ignatius here generally follows the line that Paul sketched out for the handling of this social problem. "Were you called as a slave? Do not be concerned about it. But if you are also able to gain freedom, remain all the more. For whoever was called in the Lord as a slave is the Lord's freedman. Likewise, whoever was called as free is a slave of Christ" (1 Cor 7:21–22). Both Paul and Ignatius urge slaves to persevere in their old place. Early Christianity did not want to bring a toppling social program or a revolution. It primarily wanted to convey the message of Christian love. This message of love adapted itself to the relationships of the time—not the overthrowing of slavery, but rather a humane treatment of slaves that was permeated with love of neighbor. Slaves are indeed free in the Lord. Both Paul and Ignatius proclaim this thought of a greater freedom. All differences that have value in the human realm vanish before God. The perspective of eternity is more important than temporal and earthly worldviews. The view expresses itself in Ignatius in his ardent attempts to obtain martyrdom. He now supposes that, when he is in chains and has learned to be without any wishes, slaves, who are not martyrs, are likewise able to do at least that.[40]

In early Christian communities, it was apparently usual to redeem slaves with the means of the community. Ignatius is not content with this. He fears that these freely redeemed will becomes "slaves of lust." What did Ignatius mean by this? Perhaps he means

---

40. Grant, *Ignatius*, 133.

that the freely redeemed slave, who would be easily tempted, would lead a completely idle life. Or maybe he feared that the new life would become the chief matter for the freed slave and that the struggle of faith would be a secondary matter.

Meinhold sees in this single question the principle that the pneumatic ethic supports Ignatius absolutely. Moral behavior is an expression of spiritual essence. The slave who is really filled by God "does not puff himself up." He remains in his place and does the work that has been assigned to him, if anything, even better than before.[41] Here it should be added that the one who has been captured by God's love does not aspire to higher matters. That one does not seek new positions or increased respect. This thought certainly stood in the background for Ignatius. The motif of remaining humble in love was really an important concern for Ignatius. However, one can naturally ask today whether it was justified to defend slavery in this way. Yet here the contemporary background must be considered. Relationships at that time were completely different than today. Our worldviews cannot be transferred to many centuries ago. Early Christianity was strongly defined by the imminent expectation of the Parousia. The return of Christ is approaching so the gospel should be proclaimed to as many people as possible. Therefore, it is necessary to remain spiritually awake. The community order, above all the authority, was understood to be established by God. Christians tried to be active inside this framework insofar as they did not transgress their conscience and God's commands.

In *Pol.* 1.2—5.2, Ignatius appears to hold up an early Christian "community and household code" to the believers. In chapters 4 and 5, this code presents the duties toward different statuses.[42] Before slaves, widows are mentioned who should not be without care. "After the Lord, you be there caregiver" (*Pol.* 4.1). The widows and orphans already belonged to the circle of people for whom one must particularly care in the apostolic time (Acts 6:1; 9:39, 41; 1

---

41. Meinhold, "Ethik," 62.
42. Fischer, *Die apostolischen Väter*, 221.

Tim 5:9–16; Jas 1:27).[43] In particular, it was the bishop's task to provide for the fulfillment of this Christian duty of love.

One of the most burning problems of the early Christian church was the question of how the Christian notion of love impacts the area of sexual love and marriage. On one hand, one opposed the dissolute gentile way of life; on the other hand, however, one also did not want to fall into the other highly rigorous extreme according to which virginity and singleness would have been mandatory. When Ignatius speaks of this problem in the letter addressed to Polycarp, he starts from marriage and its duties. "Tell my sisters to love the Lord and to be satisfied with their partners in flesh and spirit. Likewise, also instruct my brothers in the name of Jesus Christ to love their partners as the Lord loves the church" (*Pol.* 5.1). The Lord's love for us and our love for him is the starting point and foundation to which Ignatius always points and to which he always returns. The Pauline thoughts in Eph 5:29 and possibly 1 Cor 7:3–4 were known to Ignatius.[44] "The union occurs with the consent of the bishop so that the marriage conforms to the Lord and not to lust. Everything should happen for the honor of God" (*Pol.* 5.2). Andrén notes that an initial hint of a type of Christian marriage is to be seen.[45] Ignatius and others with him are of the mind that the marriages of believers should be defended from the beginning. Their foundation should be Christian love. Therefore, it is the bishop's task to investigate the conditions and to do everything so that the marriage "conforms to the Lord."

However, another ascetic notion is found beside this positive attitude toward marriage. Paul's response, for example, was split. He supported singleness, but did not demand it of believers. His chief policy was that everyone must decide for himself or herself in responsible freedom. However, radical ascetic aspirations to a "singleness of all who are baptized," something like those whom Paul must have encountered in Corinth, were not overcome through this. They accompanied the church's path through all of antiquity

---

43. Bauer, *Briefe*, 269; Grant, *Ignatius*, 132; Corwin, *St. Ignatius*, 241.
44. Grant, *Ignatius*, 134.
45. Andrén, *Apostoliska fäderna*, 101.

Love

and emerge again in different apocryphal traditions of the second and third centuries.[46] "If someone is able to remain in chastity for the honor of the Lord's flesh, he remains so without self-glory. If he boasts, he has been destroyed" (*Pol.* 5.2). In Meinhold's opinion, chastity stands higher in value than marriage for Ignatius, who converses here again with Paul.[47] However, hardly any conclusions can be drawn from Ignatius's remarks regarding this question. Yet he has supported the ascetic way of life and contributed to a development in this direction. Perhaps he was of the view that singleness constituted a particular form of *imitatio Christi*.[48] To this extent, then, Meinhold may be right. Ignatius's view most likely can be characterized with the modern term "friendly coexistence." Both forms of life, marriage and freely chosen singleness, are to be looked upon as equally valuable. The second way of life later develops to the ascetic ideal life of the spiritual state in the Catholic Church, to monasticism, and to the celibacy of the spiritual.

Sometimes Ignatius mentions things in his letters that do not harmonize with Christian love and destroy the relationships of Christians with one another. Envy should not dwell in them (*Rom.* 7.2) and likewise no strife. "For when no strife has invaded you that is able to afflict you, then you are living in accordance with God" (*Eph.* 8.1). Human weaknesses damage the kingdom of God and cause difficulties and hardships in human relationships. In particular, the community in Corinth was well-known for many disputes, but they also appeared elsewhere because, for example, Ignatius warns the Ephesians about it quite particularly.

Ignatius does not expressly emphasize these negative sides. However, he urges much more the things that help to build up the life of the community and to serve good relations with neighbors. He particularly advises gentleness (*Trall.* 8.1). "In response to their angry outbursts, you should be gentle" (*Eph.* 10.2). "Therefore,

---

46. von Campenhausen, *Tradition und Leben*, 147. Regarding Ignatius's attitude, Altaner says, "Die Jungfräulichkeit wird im Sinne des hl. Paulus empfohlen" (*Patrologie*, 87).

47. Meinhold, "Ethik," 60.

48. Ibid.

Faith and Love in Ignatius of Antioch

take up gentleness and renew yourselves in faith, which is the flesh of the Lord, and in love, which is the blood of Jesus Christ" (*Trall.* 8.1). Gentleness is like a weapon with which the Christian can fend off the attacks of the enemy. One can observe that the words "Love your enemies" (Matt 5:44; Luke 6:27) do not occur in Ignatius.[49] In the previously mentioned exhortations, however, the same spirit appears—the spirit of the Sermon on the Mount that demands a loving treatment even of the opponent. In Ignatius's view, gentleness is close to the chief categories of Christian faith, to faith and love.

In one place, Ignatius urges gentleness as *imitatio Dei*: therefore, be patient with one another in kindness as God is with you (*Pol.* 6.2). God treats all his creation with love. He shows unending patience when he waits on the repentance of a person. Christians must also walk with one another in this way.

Human nature is indeed also willing to practice love, but it demands gratitude and appreciation. According to Ignatius, this must not happen in Christian circles. "No one should regard the neighbor according to a fleshly manner but rather always love one another in Jesus Christ" (*Magn.* 6.2). One should suffer all things in love (*Pol.* 1.2) and show mutual love with undivided heart (*Trall.* 13.2). "If you love good disciples, you have no acknowledgement" (*Pol.* 2.1). Echoes of the word of Jesus in Luke 6:32 are found in these thoughts. "And if you love those who love you, what credit is that to you?" The command of unconditional love is found particularly in John (John 13:34; 15:12). Using Nygren's term, here is "unmotivated love" that encompasses all in a similar way and without choosing, even the enemies.

Gentleness, meekness, and love—these are the traits that are expected of a believer in dealings with their fellow human beings. On the one hand, Ignatius places them expressly in opposition to evil traits.[50] On the other hand, he appears to consider them the

---

49. Richardson, *Christianity*, 21.

50. "In a more general way agape is described as the antithesis of vainglory (κενοδοξία Phil. 1. 1), of anger, of boasting, of railing, of bad temper (*Eph.* 10.2), and of pride in office (*Smyr.* 6.1). On the contrary it is gentleness

Love

natural character traits of every Christian. He knows that people are able to love those who are pleasing and sympathetic to them of their own accord. Love for a person who is hostilely minded and attacks where possible demands a willpower and a love that exceed human measure. To participate in such a love is only possible through an encounter with God and the Redeemer, Jesus Christ.

Smyrneans 6.2 sounds like a summary that contains both the foundation of the doctrine and the demand for practical conduct.

> Watch out for those who have divergent opinions concerning the grace of Jesus Christ that has come to us as it is in opposition to the mind of God. They do not care about the duty of love, nor about widows, nor about orphans, nor about the oppressed, nor about those who are bound or (even?) those who have been freed, nor about those who are hungry or thirsty.

God's grace in Jesus forms the starting point for Ignatius. It effects salvation and by this changes the person from the ground up. The love of God that the person has experienced does not remain without reverberation. It should also be observed outside of them. Through it, they receive open eyes that necessarily have love and care for other people. Thus, love does not stay a surreal philosophical idea. Rather, it takes shape in service to the neighbor. That is to say, Christ the Lord encounters us in the neighbor.

In his letters, Ignatius brought to the Christians of his time the tasks and duties that love has to complete toward the neighbor. He has expressly pointed out the "acute" cases, the cases in which true need is concerned that required quick and effective help. The question of slavery and the question of marriage and singleness were of course time-bound, but Ignatius also tried in these problems to show the right path that has been chosen by love—in order to walk it.

(πραότης of *Tral.* 3.2; 4.2), humility (*Eph.* 10.2), kindness (*Tral.* 1.2), putting up with all men (*Pol.* 1.2), reverencing and heeding one another (*Mag.* 6.2), and holding nothing against anyone (*Tral.* 8.2)" (Richardson, *Christianity*, 21).

Faith and Love in Ignatius of Antioch

4. Love as the Foundation of Ethics

Love is the form of action by which the Christian lives and works. It constitutes the complementary part to faith, which is directed to God alone. This love comes to light particularly in relationships among Christians who have indeed become new people through baptism. It becomes evident through gentleness, mutual subordination, and charity.[51] Ignatius states the ground for such a love: because you love nothing corresponding to another life except God alone (*Eph.* 9.2; cf. *Eph.* 15.3). As was already indicated, mutual brotherly love is a characteristic trait for Ignatius and quite generally for the first church (*Eph.* 2.1; *Smyrn.* 12.1). This life in love is the person's new being, the new creation of their existence.[52] Something can be felt here of the realization of God's love for the world, for "God is love" (1 John 4:8). He does not surrender his creation; he creates a new beginning for it. Ἀγάπη is that which accomplishes it. It permeates and shapes everything.

Love stands in connection with other basic matters of Christianity, above all, with faith. In Ignatius's opinion, faith is the beginning, one can even say the starting point, for everything that comprises Christian existence. Paul also thinks similarly. Richardson exposes the difference between the views of these two. Paul emphasizes the renewing power of the Holy Spirit that works freely and without bonds and turns the hearts of believers to God. As a second-century bishop who was led more by practical interests, Ignatius sees the power of the Holy Spirit always in connection with ecclesial order. For this purpose, orthodoxy played a significant role for him. With this notion, he stands in the development between the Johannine writings and the Pastoral Epistles.[53] This expresses itself, for instance, in that obedience to the bishop is extraordinarily important for Ignatius. However, it must be considered that he understands the task of the bishop in the same way

---

51. Meinhold, "Ethik," 55.
52. Colson, "Agapè," 353.
53. Richardson, *Christianity*, 14.

Love

as he understands all tasks in the community, namely, as a service of love.

Love demonstrates itself in good works. One recognizes the Ephesians as members of the Son of God by good works (*Eph.* 4.2). Faith cannot do the works of unfaithfulness, and unfaithfulness cannot do the works of faith (*Eph.* 8.2). Faith is not complete if it does not keep itself in love. In this sense, love is the touchstone for new life and new faith. It is the principle that comes into effect in justification.[54] This notion, which is found in Torrance, gets to the heart of the matter. The shattered and broken relationship between God and the person is restored by God, out of love, by means of justification. Justification is a completely and entirely theocentric event in its character. God justifies the sinful person. He alone brings right what is in disarray. God is the one who begins and ends this work. However, justification that is rightly understood is not an event without any reverberations. It is not an event that would remain confined to the "heavenly forum." Rather, it operates clearly and recognizably in justified believers, and it is the basis both for their life of faith and also for their ethical action—their life in love.

In Ignatian theology, a close connection exists between ἀγάπη and πνεῦμα. Spirit creates love. Indeed, it *is* love.[55] Ignatius condemns the docetists, therefore, because they are indifferent with respect to love. They obviously consider purity the highest command.[56] Consequently, love is the measure with which the authenticity of the Christian life can be tested. It appears as if Ignatius has thoroughly immersed himself in the thought that Paul set down in 1 Corinthians 1 and 13. When love is missing or weak, everything else also falters.

Ignatius has therefore recognized the fundamental significance of love for the Christian faith. Alongside Pauline thought,

---

54. Torrance, *Doctrine of Grace*, 69. Nirschl emphasizes the central place of faith and love in Ignatian thought and its connection with the central event of salvation, Christ's death on the cross (*Theologie*, 112).

55. Rüsch, *Entstehung*, 69.

56. Corwin, *St. Ignatius*, 245.

it is primarily Johannine thought that has clearly influenced him strongly, either immediately or even indirectly through the Asia Minor communities in which Johannine tradition was very much alive. However, Ignatius does not hold rigidly to the biblical term ἀγάπη, but also employs the word ἔρως.[57]

Ignatian thought on this question could also be partly rooted in Old Testament piety in which the "matter of the neighbor" occupies an emphatic place.[58] On the other hand, however, one must note that Ignatius does not move markedly along the line of the Old Testament. Indeed, he considers it an astonishingly meager measure. That probably is due to the fact that he considers the entire matter of the Old Testament to be overcome through Jesus Christ.

Both holiness and love belong to the essence of God. On which of these two the stronger emphasis lies changes over the course of time. If the accent lies on holiness, the danger threatens of a legalistic Christianity that is too strongly determined by Old Testament notions. But if love stands too much in the foreground, essential moments could get lost in the picture of God, as in Marcion, for instance. It then comes to a one-sided, flattened, humanized notion of God. Ignatius has pursued neither of these directions, but it appears that the scale still leans a little more to the side of love with him. One could see a kind of protest against the Judaizers in this. Yet Ignatius always remained within more reasonable boundaries.

The difference between Christianity and Judaism can also be shown clearly in the concept of love. Observance of the Old Testament commands is characteristic for Judaism, for instance, that of the Sabbath command. The Christian faith is not a religion of the law and the letter but a religion of love and freedom. Ignatius wants to express this when he lays somewhat more emphasis on

57. "For I write to you as one who lives and desires death in love. My love (ἔρως) is crucified and no fire is in me that finds nourishment in material" (*Rom.* 7.2). Origen interprets this verse so that it here refers to the crucified Christ. But with this, the misunderstanding begins that stretches to Johann Arndt (Nygren, *Den kristna kärlekstanken*, 2.186–87).

58. Nikolainen, *Lähimmäinen Vanhassa testamentissa*, 51.

God's love. He could say with John "There is no fear in love, but perfect love casts out fear" (1 John 4:18).

Love effects harmony and union. These form an indivisible unity in Ignatian thought. They form the basis for the thought, "Therefore, the song of Jesus Christ sounds in your concord and symphonic love" (*Eph.* 4.1). However, love should effect unity not only in the community but also in the entire church and in all of Christianity—a thought that Augustine later captures: The one who does not love the unity of the church lacks the true love of God.[59]

Ignatius's ethics can be characterized as ethics of love. The daily, practical life of ἀγάπη is borne by them. They are the foundation on which Christians can build with their lives and activity. However, ethics also stand at the end of the fight of faith. According to them, nothing is superior to love because the essence of God, which is, above all, another love, reflects itself already completed in them.

---

59. Schütte (*Um die Wiedervereinigung im Glauben*, foreword) and Karrer ("Das kirchliche Amt") point out this word of Augustine about divided Christianity,

Conclusion

With this pair of words—faith and love—Ignatius has expressed the central content of the Christian faith. With precisely these words, he, perhaps as the first in Christianity, has ranged between dogmatics and ethics, between doctrine and the spiritual life on one hand and love for the neighbor and practical works on the other. Both things can be considered separately, but they form the foundation of Christianity as an indissoluble unity. It is interesting to note that the pair of words that has been mentioned also appears in Luther. Thus he says in his book *On the Freedom of a Christian* that Christians do not live for themselves but for Christ and for their neighbor—for Christ in faith and for the neighbor in love. He writes similarly in the foreword to *The German Mass* (1526), where he encapsulates the sum of the entire Christian faith "in two little things," namely, faith and love, which must be held in the heart.[1]

---

1. "Solche fragen mag man nemen aus dem unsern betbuchlin, da die drey stuck kurtz ausgelegt sind, odder selbs anders machen, bis das man die gantze summa des Christlichen verstands ynn zwey stucke als *ynn zwey secklin* fasse ym hertzen, wilchs sind glaube und liebe. Des glauben secklin habe zwey beutlin; ynn dem eynem beutlin stecke das stuck, das wyr gleuben, wie wyr durch Adams sunde alzumal verderbt, sunder und verdampt sind. . . Im andern stecke das stucklin, das wyr alle durch Jesum Christ von solchem verderbten sundlichem, verdampten wesen erlöset sind. . . Der liebe secklin habe auch zwey beutlin. Inn dem eynen stecke dis stucke, das wyr yderman sollen dienen und wolthun, wie uns Christus than hat. . .Im andern stecke das stucklin, das wyr allerley böses gerne leyden und dulden sollen" (Luther, *Werke*, 19.77). Gerhard Ebeling emphasizes the inseparability of faith and love

Conclusion

In the concepts of faith and love, the Pauline and Johannine heritage are virtually united. One can say of Ignatius that he was a genuine student of Paul, who knew his writings as well as his thoughts.[2] Paul speaks above all about faith and about the piety that comes from faith. Ignatius likewise used the first concept very often, but the second does not occur in him. It cannot be inferred from the statements that Ignatius makes about faith that he also agrees with Paul in questions concerning the piety that comes from faith. However, it is generally true that Ignatius does not achieve the same lucidity and clarity as the apostle Paul in the presentation of his thoughts about faith. John is known especially as the apostle of love. His spirit particularly shaped the Asia Minor communities in which Ignatius lived and worked. Pauline faith and Johannine love—here we have the entire heritage of the New Testament, which Ignatius has faithfully preserved and shared. Admittedly, this sharing often happened with a new accentuation that no longer meets the original sense exactly right. However, the basic matters of Christian proclamation always came clearly to expression.

Like the apostles, Ignatius places the main emphasis on Christology. Christ is true God and true man—this is the indispensable truth of Christianity and the basis of faith to which Ignatius adheres unswervingly. Here he has revealed the direction in which the solution for all the contentious questions in Christology will find their answer in the following centuries. He has also recognized and shown extraordinarily clearly the significance of unity in faith for Christianity. With this in view, one could almost regard him as a kind of forerunner to the ecumenical movement. His perception of ecclesial order aims at the unity of the church, which should be established so the community has a secure footing in

---

in Luther's thought. "So wenig wie man Person und Werk, Täter und Tat voneinander trennen kann, so wenig auch Glaube und Liebe. Es ist ein einziges Geschehen, eine einzige lebendige Wirklichkeit" (*Luther*, 179). Cf. Haikola, "Reformation und Kirchenordnung," 50ff.

2. Meinhold, "Ethik," 62; cf. Schlier, *Religionsgeschichtliche Untersuchungen*, 177.

stormy times. Ignatius has achieved here a decisive contribution for the development of the episcopacy.

In the spiritual life, Ignatius especially emphasizes the significance of prayer. However, he is here content with continuing and passing on the tradition without adding much of his own thoughts. Martyrdom is his most important desire, which he pursues with ardent zeal. He has probably stressed its significance for believers more than anyone else before or after him. Although Ignatius does not consider such a sacrifice desirable for all Christians, he still created this new ideal for following Christ with his own example that has deeply impressed both his own time and also the following generations. Ignatius has found an opportunity to be able to substantiate the unconditional commitment that is demanded by the New Testament in following Christ. However, Ignatius has simultaneously given the first impetus for the formation of two "classes," two groups in the community with different ideals of life. No longer do all Christians walk the way together, but now some choose the higher way while the majority choose the lower way to perfection. At roughly the same time, a similar development takes place in the Christian community of Syria with asceticism.[3]

The influence of Ignatius in church history cannot be described as decisive or even as epoch-making. Still, he obtained great importance in his own time. He is an important representative of the fairly little-known interim period from the New Testament to the church fathers. His statements have occasionally initiated a development and have sometimes had trend-setting influence. To this end, it should be mentioned that Polycarp (*Phil.* 13.2) and Origen (*Comm. Cant.* Prologue) appeal to him, although the latter does not construe Ignatius's thoughts properly. On one hand, Ignatius co-initiated the development of the Eastern church. It takes up Johannine thought and is carried forward by men like Melito, Irenaeus, Methodius, Marcellus, Athanasius, Gregory of Nyssa, and Cyril of Alexandria.[4] On the other hand, the Western church has

---

3. Kähler, "Nachfolge Christi," 4.1288.

4. Cf. Rackl, *Christologie*, 292. On p. 291 Rackl points out that the historical theologian Loofs is of the view that Ignatius's letters could not be too

Conclusion

also maintained basic impulses from him, particularly with regard to the emergence and structure of ecclesial office, above all, the episcopacy. Thus Karl Adam can roughly draw a line from Paul via Ignatius and Cyprian to Augustine.[5] Future development is clearly prefigured in Ignatian thought, no matter how much his ideas then may have possessed in particular and direct influence.[6] He is one of the fathers who have consolidated the Christian church because both the East and the West can invoke him. His name is cited when naming the most significant representative of the post-apostolic time. He is simultaneously an extraordinarily multifaceted Christian, bishop, pneumatic, and martyr.[7] He unites in himself those powers that diverge after him. They contradict one another and never again are combined in unity as they are still to be found in him.

In Ignatius's worldview, thoughts can be discovered that betray a foreign spirit and that bring unbiblical notions into the incipient theological reasoning of the early Christian church. For this reason, Ignatius has been held partly responsible for the process of Hellenization in the church. However, his achievement is far greater. He tried to sustain the spirit of the New Testament in all questions of faith and life. He particularly fought against the slide of Christology into gnostic thoughts and notions. For all that, he decided not only to face the dangers that he encountered but also played his part in positively giving content to the character of the Christian faith. By declaring faith and love the two fundamental things that nothing surpasses, he has emphasized the two basic concepts to which the reflection of Christian faith and any theological scholarship returns again and again.

---

highly valued. Adolf von Harnack, who does not consider Ignatius in the first edition of his historical theology, also thinks more positively about him later.

5. Laubach, "Karl Adam," 132–33.
6. Krüger, "Briefe des Ignatius," 520.
7. Meinhold, "Episkope, 324.

Bibliography

Adam, Alfred. "Bischof." In *Religion in Geschichte und Gegenwart*, edited by Kurt Galling, 3rd ed., 7 vols., 1.1301–3. Tübingen: Mohr Siebeck, 1957–65.
———. "Kirchenverfassung." In *Religion in Geschichte und Gegenwart*, edited by Kurt Galling, 3rd ed., 7 vols., 3.1533–45. Tübingen: Mohr Siebeck, 1957–65.
———. "Mystik." In *Religion in Geschichte und Gegenwart*, edited by Kurt Galling, 3rd ed., 7 vols., 4.1246–49. Tübingen: Mohr Siebeck, 1957–65.
Andrén, Olof. *De apostoliska Fäderna i svensk översättning*. Stockholm: Diakonistyrelsen, 1958.
Altaner, Berthold. *Patrologie: Leben, Schriften und Lehre der Kirchenväter*. 6th ed. Freiburg im Breisgau: Herder, 1963.
Althaus, Paul. *Der Brief an die Römer*. 6th ed. Neue Testament Deutsch 6. Göttingen: Vandenhoeck & Ruprecht, 1949.
Andresen, Carl. "Erlösung." In *Religion in Geschichte und Gegenwart*, edited by Kurt Galling, 3rd ed., 7 vols., 2.590–94. Tübingen: Mohr Siebeck, 1957–65.
Bardenhewer, Otto. *Geschichte der altkirchlichen Literatur: 1. Band. Vom Ausgange des apostolischen Zeitalters bis zum Ende des zweiten Jahrhunderts*. Freiburg im Breisgau: Herder, 1902.
Bartsch, Hans-Werner. *Gnostisches Gut und Gemeindetradition bei Ignatius von Antiochien*. Beiträge zur Förderung christlicher Theologie 2.44. Gütersloh: Bertelsmann, 1940.
———. "Ignatius von Antiochien." In *Religion in Geschichte und Gegenwart*, edited by Kurt Galling, 3rd ed., 7 vols., 3.665–67. Tübingen: Mohr Siebeck, 1957–65.
Bauer, Walter. *Die Briefe des Ignatius von Antiochia und der Polykarpbrief*. Handbuch zum Neuen Testament. Die Apostolischen Väter 2. Tübingen: Mohr, 1920.
———. *Die Rechtgläubigkeit und Ketzerei im ältesten Christentum*. Beiträge zur historischen Theologie 10. Tübingen: Mohr, 1934.
Bieder, Werner. "Zur Deutung des kirchlichen Schweigens bei Ignatius von Antiochien." *Theologische Zeitschrift* 12 (1956) 28–43.

Bibliography

Bihlmeyer, Karl. *Die apostolischen Väter, Neubearbeitung der Funkschen Ausgabe.* 2nd ed. Tübingen: Mohr Siebeck, 1956.

Bousset, Wilhelm. *Kyrios Christos: Geschichte des Christusglaubens von Anfängen des Christentums bis Irenaeus.* 5th ed. Göttingen: Vandenhoeck & Ruprecht, 1965.

Bultmann, Rudolf. "Ignatius und Paulus." In *Studia paulina in honorem Johannis de Zwaan septuagenarii*, edited by J. N. Sevenster and W. C. Van Unnik, 37–51. Haarlem: Bohn, 1953.

Camelot, Pierre-Thomas. *Ignace d'Antioche, Polycarpe de Smyrne: Lettres. Martyre de Polycarpe.* 2nd ed. Sources chrétiennes 10. Paris: Cerf, 1951.

Campenhausen, Hans Freiherr von. *Die Idee des Martyriums in der alten Kirche.* 2nd ed. Göttingen: Vandenhoeck & Ruprecht, 1964.

———. *Tradition und Leben, Kräfte der Kirchengeschichte: Aufsätze und Vorträge.* Tübingen: Mohr, 1960.

Colson, Jean. "Agapè chez Saint-Ignace d'Antioche." In *Studia Patristica 3 (Texte und Untersuchungen zur Geschichte der altchristlichen Literatur 78)*, edited by Frank Leslie Cross, 341–53. Berlin: Akademie, 1961.

Corwin, Virginia. *St. Ignatius and Christianity in Antioch.* Yale Publications in Religion 1. New Haven: Yale University Press, 1960.

Crone, Gerhard. *Ignatius von Antiochien: Briefe.* 2nd ed. Aschendorffs Sammlung lateinischer und griechischer Klassiker: Lesehefte. Münster in Westfalia: Aschendorff, 1958.

Downey, Glanville. *A History of Antioch in Syria: From Seleucus to the Arab Conquest.* Princeton: Princeton University Press, 1961.

Ebeling, Gerhard. *Luther: Einführung in sein Denken.* Tübingen: Mohr, 1965.

Fischer, Joseph A. *Die apostolischen Väter.* Schriften des Urchristentums 1. Darmstadt: Wissenschaftliche Buchgesellschaft, 1956.

Funk, Francis Xavier and Karl Bihlmeyer. *Kirchengeschichte auf Grund des Lehrbuches von F. X. von Funk: Erster Teil: Das christliche Altertum.* 9th ed. Paderborn: Schöningh, 1931.

Goltz, Eduard von der. *Ignatius von Antiochien als Christ und Theologe.* Texte und Untersuchungen zur Geschichte der altchristlichen Literatur 12.3. Leipzig: Hinrichs, 1894.

Goppelt, Leonard. *Die apostolische und nachapostolische Zeit.* 2nd ed. Die Kirche in ihrer Geschichte 1. Göttingen: Vandenhoeck & Ruprecht, 1966.

Grant, Robert M. *Ignatius of Antioch.* The Apostolic Fathers: A New Translation and Commentary 4. Camden, NJ: Thomas Nelson, 1966.

Gulin, Eelis Gideon. *Roomalaiskirje.* Suomen eksegeettisen seuran julkaisuja 19. Helsinki: Otava, 1959.

Haag, Herbert. "Die Buchwerdung des Wortes Gottes in der heiligen Schrift." In *Mysterium salutis: Grundriß heilsgeschichtlicher Dogmatik*, edited by Johannes Feiner and Magnus Löhrer, 5 vols., 1.289–427. Einsiedeln: Benyiger, 1965–76.

Bibliography

Haikola, Lauri. "Reformation und Kirchenordnung: Erlass herausgegeben von dem Komitee der XIX ordentlichen Kirchenversammlung für die Erneuerung der kirchlichen Gesetzgebung und Verwaltung." 1967.

Hamman, Adalbert. "Die Trinität in der Liturgie und im christlichen Leben." In *Mysterium salutis: Grundriß heilsgeschichtlicher Dogmatik*, edited by Johannes Feiner and Magnus Löhrer, 5 vols., 2.132–44. Einsiedeln: Benyiger, 1965–76.

Harnack, Adolf von. *Entstehung und Entwicklung der Kirchenverfassung und des Kirchenrechts in den zwei ersten Jahrhunderten*. Leipzig: Hinrichs, 1910.

Harrison, P. N. *Polycarp's Two Epistles to the Philippians*. Cambridge: Cambridge University Press, 1936.

Hauck, Friedrich. *Die Briefe des Jakobus, Petrus, Judas und Johannes: Kirchenbriefe*. 5th ed. Neue Testament Deutsch, neues Göttinger Bibelwerk 10. Göttingen: Vandenhoeck & Ruprecht, 1949.

Heilmann, Alfons, and Heinrich Kraft. *Texte der Kirchenväter*. 5 vols. Munich: Kösel, 1963–66.

Hutten, Kurt. *Die Glaubenswelt des Sektierers: Das Sektentum als antireformatische Konfession—sein Anspruch und seine Tragödie*. Furche Studien 24. Hamburg: Im Furche, 1957.

Joest, Wilfried. "Rechtfertigung: II. Dogmengeschichtlich: 1. Bis zur Reformation und im nachreformatorischen Katholizismus." In *Religion in Geschichte und Gegenwart*, edited by Kurt Galling, 3rd ed., 7 vols., 5.828–34. Tübingen: Mohr Siebeck, 1957–65.

Johansson, Nils. "Till frågan om ämbetets kontinuitet i fornkyrkan." In *Till Bo Giertz*, edited by Carl Henrik Martling, et al., 155–78. Uppsala: Merkantiltryckeriet, 1965.

Karrer, Otto. "Das kirchliche Amt in katholischer Sicht." In *Theologie heute: Eine Vortragsreihe des Bayerischen Rundfunks*, edited by Leonhard Reinisch, 3rd ed., 115–30. Munich: Beck, 1963.

Kähler, Ernst. "Nachfolge Christi." In *Religion in Geschichte und Gegenwart*, edited by Kurt Galling, 3rd ed., 7 vols., 4.1288–92. Tübingen: Mohr Siebeck, 1957–65.

Kelly, J. N. D. *Early Christian Doctrines*. 3rd ed. London: Black, 1965.

Kettler, F. H. "Trinität III: Dogmengeschichtlich." In *Religion in Geschichte und Gegenwart*, edited by Kurt Galling, 3rd ed., 7 vols., 6.1025–26. Tübingen: Mohr Siebeck, 1957–65.

Knopf, Rudolf. *Das nachapostolische Zeitalter: Geschichte der christlichen Gemeinden vom Beginn der Flavierdynastie bis zum Ende Hadrians*. Tübingen: Mohr, 1905.

Krüger, Gustav. "Briefe des Ignatius." In *Neutestamentliche Apokryphen*, edited by Edgar Hennecke, 2nd ed., 518–40. Tübingen: Mohr, 1924.

Laubach, Jacob. "Karl Adam." In *Theologen unserer Zeit: Eine Vortragsreihe des Bayerischen Rundfunks*, edited by Leonhard Reinisch, 132–33. Munich: Beck, 1965.

Bibliography

Lauha, Aarre. *Katoliset kirjeet*. Suomalainen Uuden testamentin selitys 11. Helsinki: Kirjapaja, 1956.

———. *Otti orjan muodon: Kenosis-ajatus Uudessa testamentissa*. Suomen eksegeettisen seuran julkaisuja 1. Helsinki: Suomen eksegeettinen seura, 1939.

Loewenlich, Walther von. *Die Geschichte der Kirche: Altertum und Mittelalter*. Siebenstern-Taschenbuch 2. Munich: Siebenstern, 1964.

Lietzmann, Hans. *Geschichte der alten Kirche*. 4th ed. 4 vols. Berlin: de Gruyter, 1961.

Lightfoot, J. B. *The Apostolic Fathers: Clement, Ignatius, and Polycarp: Revised Texts with Introductions, Notes, Dissertations, and Translations*. 2nd ed. 5 vols. London: MacMillan, 1889–91.

Lohse, Bernhard. "Ignatius von Antiochien." In *Evangelisches Kirchenlexikon: Kirchlich-theologisches Handwörterbuch*, edited by Heinz Brunotte and Otto Weber. Göttingen: Vandenhoeck & Ruprecht, 1956–61.

Luther, Martin. *D. Martin Luthers Werke: Kritische Gesamtausgabe*. 120 vols. Weimar: Hermann Böhlaus Nachfolger, 1883–2009.

Maurer, Christian. *Ignatius von Antiochien und das Johannesevangelium*. Abhandlungen zur Theologie des Alten und Neuen Testaments 18. Zürich: Zwingli-Verlag, 1949.

Meinhold, Peter. "Episkope–Pneumatiker–Märtyrer: Zur Deutung der Selbstaussagen des Ignatius von Antiochien." *Saeculum* 14 (1963) 308–24.

———. "Die Ethik des Ignatius von Antiochien." *Historisches Jahrbuch* 77 (1958) 50–62.

Molland, Einar. "The Heretics Combatted by Ignatius of Antioch." *The Journal of Ecclesiastical History* 5 (1954) 1–6.

Nikolainen, Aimo T. *Lähimmäinen Vanhassa testamentissa*. Suomen eksegeettisen seuran julkaisuja 2. Helsinki: Otava, 1939.

Nirschl, Joseph. *Die Theologie des heiligen Ignatius des Apostelschülers und Bischofs von Antiochien aus seinen Briefen dargestellt*. Mainz: Franz Kirchheim, 1880.

Norden, Eduard. *Die antike Kunstprosa vom 6. Jahrhundert vor Christus bis in die Zeit der Renaissance*. 2nd ed. 2 vols. Leipzig: Teubner, 1909.

Nygren, Anders. *Agape and Eros*. London: SPCK, 1953.

———. *Den kristna kärlekstanken genom tiderna: Eros och agape*. 2nd ed. 2 parts. Stockholm: Svenska Kyrkans Diakonistyrelses Bokförlag, 1947.

Pannenberg, Wolfhart. *Grundzüge der Christologie*. Gütersloh: Gütersloher Verlagshaus, 1964.

Quasten, Johannes. *Patrology*. 4th ed. 4 vols. Utrecht: Spectrum, 1966.

Rackl, Michael. *Die Christologie des heiligen Ignatius, nebst einer Voruntersuchung: Die Echtheit der sieben ignatianischen Briefe verteidigt gegen Daniel Völter*. Freiburger Theologische Studien 14. Freiburg im Breisgau: Herder, 1914.

Bibliography

Rahner, Karl, and Karl Lehmann. "Kerygma und Dogma." In *Mysterium salutis: Grundriß heilsgeschichtlicher Dogmatik*, edited by Johannes Feiner and Magnus Löhrer, 5 vols., 1.622–703. Einsiedeln: Benyiger, 1965–76.

Richardson, Cyril Charles. *The Christianity of Ignatius of Antioch*. New York: Columbia University Press, 1935.

Riesenfeld, Harald. "Reflections on the Style and the Theology of St. Ignatius of Antioch." In *Studia Patristica* 4 (*Texte und Untersuchungen zur Geschichte der altchristlichen Literatur* 79), edited by Frank Leslie Cross, 312–22. Berlin: Akademie, 1961.

Roloff, Jürgen. *Apostolat—Verkündigung—Kirche: Ursprung, Inhalt und Funktion des kirchlichen Apostelamtes nach Paulus, Lukas und den Pastoralbriefen*. Gütersloh: Gütersloher Verlagshaus, 1965.

Rüsch, Theodor. *Die Entstehung der Lehre vom Heiligen Geist bei Ignatius von Antiochien, Theophilus von Antiocheia und Irenäus von Lyon*. Studien zur Dogmengeschichte und systematischen Theologie 2. Zurich: Zwingli, 1952.

Scheffczyk, Leo. "Das Werden des Trinitätsdogmas im Frühchristentum." In *Mysterium salutis: Grundriß heilsgeschichtlicher Dogmatik*, edited by Johannes Feiner and Magnus Löhrer, 5 vols., 2.147–220. Einsiedeln: Benyiger, 1965–76.

Schlier, Heinrich. *Religionsgeschichtliche Untersuchungen zu den Ignatiusbriefen*. Beihefte zur Zeitschrift für die neutestamentliche Wissenschaft 8. Gießen: Töpelmann, 1929.

Schütte, Heinz. *Um die Wiedervereinigung im Glauben*. Essen: Fredebeul und Koenen, 1958.

Seeberg, Reinhold. *Lehrbuch der Dogmengeschichte: Die Anfänge des Dogmas im nachapostolischen und altkatholischen Zeitalter*. 5th ed. Basel: Schwabe, 1960.

———. *Lehrbuch der Dogmengeschichte: Die Dogmenbildung in der alten Kirche*. 5th ed. Basel: Schwabe, 1960.

Sormunen, Eino. *Dogmihistoria: Kristillisten oppien ja uskontouuksien vaiheet*. Luterilaisen kirjallisuuden säätiön julkaisuja 5. Helsinki: Kirjapaja, 1952.

———. *Pseudo-Dionysius Areopagita ja hänen uusplatonilaisen mystagogiansa pääpiirteet*. Helsinki: Tekijä, 1934.

Stenroth, Osvald. *Apostolisten isien kirjat sekä eräitä muita vanhimmam kristillisen kirjallisuuden tuotteita Uuden Testamentin ulkopuelelta*. Suomalaisen teologisen Kirjallisuusseuran Julkaisuja 17. Helsinki: Suomalaisen teologisen Kirjallisuusseuran, 1928.

Tarvainen, Olavi. "Apostolisten isien käsitys Kristuksen seuraamisesta." *Teologinen aikakauskirja* (1940).

Tinsley, E. J. "The *imitatio Christi* in the Mysticism of St. Ignatius of Antioch." In *Studia Patristica* 2 (*Texte und Untersuchungen zur Geschichte der altchristlichen Literatur* 64), edited by Frank Leslie Cross, 553–60. Berlin: Akademie, 1957.

Bibliography

Torrance, Thomas F. *The Doctrine of Grace in the Apostolic Fathers*. Grand Rapids: Eerdmans, 1960.
Vial, Jean-Louis. *Ignace d'Antioche*. Paris: Les éditions ouvrières, 1956.
Wolf, Ernst. "Christentum." In *Religion in Geschichte und Gegenwart*, edited by Kurt Galling, 3rd ed., 7 vols., 1.1696. Tübingen: Mohr Siebeck, 1957–65.
Zahn, Theodor. *Ignatius von Antiochien*. Gotah: Perthes, 1873.

Author Index

Adam, Alfred, 39, 41–42, 67
Altaner, Berthold, 41, 43, 79
Althaus, Paul, 65
Andrén, Olof, 21, 38, 43, 74, 78
Andresen, Carl, 68

Bardenhewer, Otto, xxiv, 43, 47
Bartsch, Hans-Werner, xxv–xxvi, 14, 27, 29–30, 68
Bauer, Walter, 3, 11, 16, 21, 37, 40–42, 62, 66, 78
Bayer, Oswald, xv
Bergamelli, Ferdinando, x
Bieder, Werner, xxvi, 40
Bihlmeyer, Karl, xxvi, 41
Bonhoeffer, Dietrich, ix
Bousset, Wilhelm, 19, 25
Bower, Richard A., xi
Brent, Allen, xiv, xvii
Bultmann, Rudolf, xxvi, 54–55, 69

Camelot, Pierre-Thomas, 23
Campenhausen, Hans Freiherr von, xxi, xxvi, 59–60, 62, 64, 68, 79
Chadwick, Henry, xxi, 40
Colson, Jean, x, 1, 82
Corwin, Virginia, xxvi, 5, 17, 22, 27, 30, 57–58, 73, 78, 83
Crone, Gerhard, xxvi

Donahue, Paul J., xvii

Downey, Glanville, xxiii, xxvi, 32, 35, 60

Ebeling, Gerhard, xv, 86–87
Elliot, Mark W., x

Fischer, Joseph A., xxvi, 14, 24, 40, 43–44, 46, 49–50, 61, 64, 74, 77
Foster, Paul, xiii
Funk, Francis Xavier, 41

Genouillac, Henri de, xii
Gilliam, Paul R., xvi
Goltz, Eduard von der, x, xxv, 4, 55, 60
Goppelt, Leonard, 11
Grant, Robert M., xi, xxiv, xxvi, 2–3, 5, 7, 17–18, 21, 40, 53, 57, 60–61, 63–65, 73–74, 76, 78
Gulin, Eelis Gideon, 65

Haag, Herbert, 49
Haikola, Lauri, 87
Hamman, Adalbert, 63, 69–70
Harnack, Adolf von, 43, 45, 89
Harrison, P. N., xvi, 50, 73
Hauck, Friedrich, 20
Hays, Richard, xii
Heilmann, Alfons, xxiii, 48
Hill, Charles E., xiii

Author Index

Hübner, Reinhard M., xvii
Hutten, Kurt, 10–11

Inge, William R., xiii
Isacson, Mikael, xi

Joest, Wilfried, 55
Johansson, Nils, 45–46
Joly, Robert, xvi

Kähler, Ernst, 88
Karrer, Otto, 85
Kelly, J. N. D., 19
Kettler, F. H., 26
Knopf, Rudolf, 41, 44, 47
Kraft, Heinrich, xxiii, 48
Krüger, Gustav, 58, 89

Laubach, Jacob, 89
Lauha, Aarre, 20, 24
Lechner, Thomas, xvii
Lehmann, Karl, 46
Lietzmann, Hans, 7, 24
Lieu, Judith M., xiii
Lightfoot, J. B., xxiv–xxv, 7, 13–16, 18, 22, 27, 40, 44, 63–64, 66, 68
Lindemann, Andreas, xiii
Loewenlich, Walther von, 51, 59, 65
Lohse, Bernhard, 42
Luther, Martin, xv–xvi, xxi, 8, 57, 75, 86–87

Marshall, John W., xvii
Martin, Jose Pablo, xi
Maurer, Christian, xxvi
Meinhold, Peter, xxi, xxvi, 6, 18, 21, 40, 45, 48–49, 56, 77, 79, 82, 87, 89
Molland, Einar, 14–16, 54
Morgan, Teresa, xii
Myllykoski, Matti, xvii

Nagel, Titus, xiii

Nikolainen, Aimo T., 84
Nirschl, Joseph, 83
Norden, Eduard, xxiv
Nygren, Anders, 3, 19, 57, 80, 84

Pannenberg, Wolfhart, 23, 26–28

Quasten, Johannes, 34, 42–44

Rackl, Michael, xxiv, xxvi, 17–18, 20, 25, 27, 49, 59, 88
Rahner, Karl, 46
Richardson, Cyril Charles, xxvi, 4–5, 30, 43, 66, 80–82
Riesenfeld, Harald, xxv, 13, 17, 55
Robinson, Thomas A., xiv
Roloff, Jürgen, 41, 48
Rüsch, Theodor, xxvi, 5, 19, 27, 30–31, 44, 56–57, 83

Scheffczyk, Leo, 70
Schlier, Heinrich, xxv, 6, 23–24, 27, 55, 67–68, 87
Schoedel, William R., xi, xvi
Schütte, Heinz, 85
Seeberg, Reinhold, 4, 15, 26–27, 44
Snyder, Graydon F., xi
Sormunen, Eino, xxi, 28, 48
Stenroth, Osvald, 74
Strawbridge, Jennifer R., xiii

Tarvainen, Olavi, ix–xix, 68
Tinsley, E. J., 58
Torrance, Thomas F., xxvi, 34, 58, 83
Trebilco, Paul, xiii

Vall, Gregory, xi
Vial, Jean-Louis, 3, 33

Wallis, Ian G., xiii
Whitenton, Michael R., x
Wolf, Ernst, 18

Author Index

Zahn, Theodor, xxiv–xxvi, 11, 14–15, 44

Zañartu, Sergio, xi

Ancient Document Index

Old Testament/Hebrew Bible

Psalms
23	60
32:9 (HB 33:9)	17

Proverbs
3:34	70

Isaiah
5	12
5:26	17
52:5	17
59:17	7

Malachi
1:11	63

Apocrypha

Wisdom of Solomon
7:29–30	17
18:14	17

Pseudepigrapha

Jubilees
	17

New Testament

Matthew
1:2–16	21
5:11–12	61
5:44	80
7:15	12
10:16	12
12:33	5
15:13	12
16:18	48
16:23	71
20:28	45
24:4	12
24:13	5

Luke
3:23–38	21
6:27	80
6:32	80
10:3	12
11:47–51	61

John

1:3	28
1:14	20
3:16	6
5:19	29
5:30	29
8:28	29
12:49	29
13:34	80
15:12	80

Acts

6:1	77
7:51–52	61
9:39	77
9:41	77
20:18	68

Romans

2:22	12
3:25	19
5–8	56
5:9	19
12:1	65

1 Corinthians

1	83
1:10–17	10
4:13	74
6:9	12
7:3–4	78
7:5	50
7:21–22	76
13	83
14:33	47
15:8–9	xiv
15:9	73

Galatians

1:1	37
5:1	15

Ephesians

1:7	19
2:13	19
4:4–6	30
5:2	3
5:5	12
5:29	78
6:13–17	7

Philippians

2:3	73
2:5–11	24

Colossians

1:16	2
1:20	19–20
2:8–10	20
2:20	10
4:5	39

1 Thessalonians

4:12	39
5:17	50

1 Timothy

2:5	20
3:7	39
5:9–16	78
6:20	20

Titus

3:10	11

James

1:27	78
4:6	70

1 Peter

5:5	70

1 John

1:7	19

4:1–3	20	**Canons of the**	
4:2	20	**Ecumenical Councils**	
4:8	3, 82		
4:18	2, 85		
5:18	6	Nicaea	
		18	xv, 72
2 John		19	xv, 72
7	20		
		Chalcedon	
Revelation		15	xv, 72
2–3	42		
		1 Clement	
		5	74
Dead Sea Scrolls		42	41
		44	41
Habakkuk Commentary			
(1QpHab)		*3 Corinthians*	
	17	5	21
Damascus Document (CD)		Ignatius	
	17	*Ephesians*	
		1.1	x, 3, 59
		1.2	66
Greco-Roman		1.3	59
Writings		2.1	82
		2.2	36
Acta Archelai		3.1	72
	6	4.1	45, 85
		4.2	32, 83
		5.1	33
		5.2	53
Early Christian		5.3	36, 70
Writings		6.1	11, 35, 39–40
		7.2	24–25
Augustine		8.1	64, 74, 79
De unitate ecclesiae		8.2	83
2	xv	9.1–2	11
		9.1	x–xi, xvi, 6, 19
		9.2	82
		10.1	50–51, 53
		10.2	53, 79–81
		11.1	29, 59
		12.2	51, 68

Ancient Document Index

13.1–2	2	*Trallians*	
13.2	2	1.2	59
14.1–2	x, 17	2.2	36, 45
14.1	xi, 2	3.1	36, 45
14.2	5	3.2	39
15.1	17, 26	4.1	71
15.2	39	5.2	2, 72
15.3	2, 82	6.1	xi, 11–12
16.1–2	11–12	6.2	21
17	11	7.1–2	45
17.2	xi	7.1	46
18.1	xi	8.1	x–xi, 6, 79–80
18.2	21, 25	8.2	17
19.1–3	23–24	9.1	20–21
19.1	2	9.2	22
20.1	x, xiii	10	22
20.2	xi, 21, 36, 56	12.1	xv
21.2	xiii–xv, 52, 62, 73	12.2	53
		12.3	51, 62
Magnesians		13.1	xiv–xv, 52, 74
1.1	34, 75	13.2	80
1.2	x, 2, 3, 30	13.3	xiii, 51–52, 64
5.2	x		
6.1	x, 24, 31, 36, 45	*Romans*	
6.2	35, 80	inscr.	x, 42
7.1–2	29	1.1–2	51
7.1	xi, 2, 36, 45	1.1	52
8–11	14	1.2	51, 63
8.1	15–16	2.1	51, 64
8.2	xi, 26, 28, 39, 61	2.2	32, 64
9.1	15–16	3.2	xiii, 51
9.2	16, 59	4.1–2	63–64
10.1–3	18	4.2	51
10.1	16	4.3	74
10.2	xi, 15	5.1	54, 61
10.3	14	5.2	62
11.1	71	5.3	51, 59, 72
13.1–2	46	6.1	51
13.1	x, 3, 45–46	6.3	59
13.2	36	7.2	79, 84
14–15	xv	7.3	21
14.1	xiv, 51–52, 73	9.1–10.2	xv
15	xi, 31	9.1	52
		9.2	xiv, 73

9.3	75	9.1	36
		9.2	57, 67
Philadelphians		10.1	xv, 53
inscr.	xi, 45	10.2	2
1.1	37, 39–40, 71	11.1–12.1	xv
1.2	32	11.1	xiv, 50, 73
2.1	12, 36	11.3	50
2.2	31	12.1	57, 82
3.1	12	12.2	45
3.3	13	13.1	3
4	32–33	13.2	x, 57
5.1	51		
7.1	45	*Polycarp*	
7.2	11, 30, 36, 59	1.2–5.2	77
8.1	11, 57	1.2	2, 30, 57, 80–81
8.2	xii–xiii, 54	1.3	50
9.2	x, 3, 21	2.1	80
10.1–11.2	xv	3.1	12
10.1	50	3.2	24–25
11.1	57	4.1	37, 77
11.2	x, 75	4.3	76
		5.1	78
Smyrneans		5.2	37, 78–79
inscr.	x, 3	6.1	32, 45, 74
1.1–2	xii	6.2	x, 7, 80
1.1	x, 3, 21, 25	7.1	50
1.2	17, 21	7.2–8.2	xv
2	21–22	7.2	57
3.2	22		
3.3	22	Origen	
4.1	53	*Commentary on the Song of Songs*	
4.2	60, 69		
5.1	16	prol.	88
6.1	x–xi, xiv, 1, 19, 56, 72		
6.2	81	Polycarp	
7.1	50	*Philippians*	
7.2	16	13	49
8.1	38, 45	13.2	88
8.2	37, 44		

www.ingramcontent.com/pod-product-compliance
Lightning Source LLC
Chambersburg PA
CBHW071623170426
43195CB00038B/2078